simple ways to success

british

Mark Hix

photography by Jason Lowe

First published exclusively for J Sainsbury plc in 2003 by Quadrille Publishing Limited
Alhambra House 27-31, Charing Cross Road, London WC2H OLS

Editorial director Jane O'Shea **Creative director** Helen Lewis
Managing editor Janet Illsley **Art direction and design** Vanessa Courtier
Photographer Jason Lowe **Food stylists** Mark Hix and Stuart Gillies **Props stylist** Jane Campsie
Editor Lewis Esson **Production** Vincent Smith and Beverley Richardson

Cataloguing in Publication Data: a catalogue record for this book is available from the British Library.

ISBN 1 84400 050 8
Printed in China

contents

NOTES

All spoon measures are level unless otherwise stated:
1 teaspoon = 5 ml spoon; 1 tablespoon = 15 ml spoon.

Where stock is specified, use either homemade stock or stock made
with good quality stock cubes.

Use fresh herbs unless dried herbs are suggested.

Use freshly ground black pepper unless otherwise stated.

Free-range eggs are recommended and large eggs should be used
except where a different size is specified.

Recipes which feature raw or lightly cooked eggs should be avoided
by anyone who is pregnant or in a vulnerable health group.

introduction

Over the last two decades, we have rediscovered the pleasures of eating and cooking in this country. In general, we have become much more knowledgeable about all sorts of food – thanks to food writers, TV chefs, supermarkets and specialist food stores, regular foreign holidays and the flurry of adventurous new restaurants. Until recently, at least, this revolution has largely been based on foreign cuisines and newly imported ingredients from afar. Many of our own traditional fruits and vegetables, rare breeds of cattle and poultry, and artisan food products like cheeses and hams have been overlooked in all of this. Now, fortunately, our finest indigenous foods are being revived and reintroduced into our diets, in the wake of our rediscovery of cooking in general.

Old-fashioned vegetables that fell out of our ken, like Jerusalem artichokes and sea kale, are reappearing in our shops. Forgotten varieties of fruits, like quince, and rare types of apples are now being marketed anew – supermarkets sometimes boasting a dozen different types alongside the Golden Delicious and Granny Smiths. Restaurants are also using tastier, less expensive cuts of meat, once designated as poor man's food while the rich had the prime cuts. Shins, shanks and necks are now commonplace on most restaurant menus in some form or another, and are now in turn offered by butchers and supermarkets for the public to recreate those dishes. Finding such things on restaurant menus has also given people the confidence to buy cuts like rib-eye steaks instead of sirloins, and hocks instead of gammon.

Many British puddings have an interesting history of some kind, often linked to royalty or other famous old households or institutions, conjuring up images of grand kitchens in full swing, preparing dishes that we have almost forgotten. British puddings have a reputation for being stodgy, but given a fresh approach they can be full of flavour and still totally comforting. And what could be better than serving them with some thick Jersey cream or clotted cream?

People are again waking up to the fact that British food isn't all that bad ... that there is a British cuisine of which we can not only be justifiably proud, but one that we can relish, explore and develop. I often come across an old dish that I have either forgotten about or never heard of in the first place, and can't wait to get it on the menu. Where appropriate, I give these wonderful old ideas a fresh modern twist to bring them totally up to date. For instance, as ordinary mushrooms can be a bit dull and tasteless, I add wild mushrooms, like girolles or chanterelles, ceps or pieds de mouton, to Kentish pudding for a much more exciting taste. This is the approach I have taken with the recipes in this book, as some of the ingredients I value for their flavour today were not widely available in Britain when these dishes where originally created.

Nowadays, there aren't many ingredients we can't get our hands on – thanks to supermarkets becoming increasingly adventurous, farmers' markets and specialist suppliers. The passion for British food is creeping back into our homes and on to our tables. In writing this book, my aim is to help you in this exciting process of rediscovery.

guide to British ingredients

In Britain we are actually blessed with some of the finest ingredients in the world, although lots of them don't always find their way into our normal shopping territory and we may have to go searching for them. We may also take for granted certain indigenous foods that stare us in the face daily. For example, Scotland has an international reputation for some of the finest beef in the world, some of our best wild mushrooms come from the Highlands, and Scottish seafood, like oysters, scallops and langoustines (Dublin Bay prawns), are prized and exported all over the world.

However, we rarely put things into our shopping trolley unless we've tried them before and enjoyed them. We all know what to do with most of our common ingredients but rarely deviate into experimentation, even if it's a simple concoction like colcannon (page 138), or flavouring our mash with mustard to go with sausages. Vegetables like celeriac and Jerusalem artichokes often sit on the shelves until they have passed their sell-by dates because few of us know how to tackle their knobbly exteriors.

If, like me, you enjoy living off the land, you can enjoy your own wild mushrooms when in season, although you need to know what you are picking, as well as things like samphire and other sea vegetables like sea beet. It makes you appreciate the seasons for what they are and you also come to understand how our weather can affect the growth of produce so much. These days, sadly, you rarely see families armed with baskets picking wild blackberries and other soft fruits in the woods; if you do get the chance, though, take the kids for a walk with the basket, show them how food really grows and get them to pick their own supper.

Whenever I hear the phrase 'in season', I automatically take more interest, as it's a joy to be offered something on the menu that uses a native ingredient in its prime. In our restaurants we keep our menus as seasonal as possible to make life interesting for both our customers and chefs. When you get customers asking when the elvers or gull's eggs are starting, you know you are sending out that seasonal message on the menu. Although nowadays most ingredients are available all year round, flown in from some part of the world or another, food in season in your own neck of the woods usually has more flavour and is certainly almost always cheaper.

Tender green asparagus is one of the classic English vegetables and I just can't wait for May to come when it will be with us for 4–6 weeks, depending on how temperamental the weather is. It's the same for most of our fruit and veg – the seasons can be as long or short as the weather allows them, but even so we have amazing ingredients throughout the year. The arrival of the first Jersey Royal potatoes informs us that spring is here and it's going to get warmer, hopefully. The good old English strawberry is, of course, symbolic of midsummer, with Wimbledon and sunshine.

With our increasing awareness of our food heritage, we are once again enthusiastically marking the passage of the year by anticipating the arrival of seasonal produce ... fresh spring lamb, lush summer berries, autumnal game birds, chestnuts and wild mushrooms, and the root vegetables and Brussels sprouts of winter. There is also a natural synergy of ingredients, in that foods in season at the same time usually work particularly well together, like lamb and broad beans, or apples and blackberries.

seasonal availability

To help you make the most of our seasonal produce, I have listed British ingredients in the months in which I find they are at their best to eat.

January: sprats, Cornish cauliflower, forced rhubarb

February: purple sprouting broccoli, spring shallot shoots, Brussels sprouts, celeriac, leeks

March: new-season's garlic, garlic shoots, nettles, sea kale

April: elvers, razor clams, guinea fowl and pheasant eggs, Jersey Royal potatoes, St George's mushrooms, wild sorrel

May: crabs, gull's eggs, asparagus, peas, broad beans, watercress

June: wild salmon, sea trout, new-season's carrots, sprouting broccoli, radishes, sea beet, wild fennel, horseradish, cultivated strawberries, Discovery apples, chamomile, elderflowers

July: samphire, sweetcorn, tomatoes, runner beans, lettuce, gooseberries, strawberries, raspberries, cherries, purslane, thyme

August: cucumbers, Scottish girolles, gooseberries, pears, wild strawberries, blackcurrants, Dorset blueberries, tayberries, loganberries, sloes

September: beetroot, chard, pumpkins, ceps, pears, field mushrooms, crab apples, elderberries, blackberries

October: native oysters, mussels, turbot, chanterelles, oyster mushrooms, puff balls, Cox's orange pippins, hazelnuts, chestnuts, rowanberries, Kentish cob nuts, walnuts

November: parsnips, swede, Jerusalem artichokes

December: goose, quince

seasonal availability of game birds

Grouse: August 12 – December 10

Partridge: September 1 – February 1

Pheasant: October 1 – February 1

Snipe: August 12 – January 31

Mallard: September 1 – February 20

Widgeon: September 1 – February 20

1 soups

creamed onion soup with cider

Here is the British answer to classic French onion soup. The addition of cider sweetens the onions and gives the soup a mellow flavour, quite unlike its French counterpart.

SERVES 4–6
1 tablespoon vegetable oil
5 medium onions, peeled and thinly sliced
1 teaspoon chopped thyme leaves
good knob of butter
1 tablespoon plain flour
125ml (4fl oz) dry cider
1 litre (1³/₄ pints) vegetable stock
2 tablespoons double cream
sea salt and freshly ground black or
  white pepper

1 Heat the oil in a heavy-based pan, then add the sliced onions and thyme. Cover and cook gently for about 10 minutes, until the onions are soft but not coloured.

2 Add the butter and allow to melt, then sprinkle in the flour and stir over a low heat for a minute or so. Slowly add the cider, stirring constantly, then gradually add the vegetable stock and season with salt and pepper. Bring to the boil and simmer for 45 minutes.

3 Stir in the cream and check the seasoning. Ladle into warm soup plates and serve.

watercress soup with goat's cheese

Watercress farms are dotted throughout Hampshire and Dorset, but unfortunately, most of their wonderful produce ends up garnishing roasts and grills, often to be left on the plate. This fresh-tasting soup is a great way to appreciate the true flavour of this underused peppery salad leaf. Like most soups and sauces that are made with leafy green herbs, brief cooking and quick chilling are essential to preserve the delicate flavour of the watercress. Try to buy soft creamy goat's cheese, which means that it is fresh not matured. You can serve this soup hot or cold.
Illustrated on previous page

SERVES 4–6
250g (9oz) watercress, washed
1 tablespoon vegetable or corn oil
1 leek, trimmed, roughly chopped and rinsed
1 small floury potato, about 80–100g (3–3½oz),
  peeled and diced
1.2 litres (2 pints) vegetable stock
100g (3½oz) soft English goat's cheese
sea salt and freshly ground black pepper

1 Cut the main stalks from the watercress and reserve. Heat the oil in a pan, add the leek and potato, cover and cook gently for about 10 minutes until soft, without allowing them to colour. Add the vegetable stock, season with salt and pepper and bring to the boil. Simmer for 10 minutes, then add the watercress stalks and simmer for another 5 minutes.

2 Remove from the heat and add the watercress sprigs. Whiz the soup in a blender or using a hand-held blender until smooth, then pass through a fine-meshed sieve into a clean pan. If serving hot, reheat the soup briefly and season again with salt and pepper, if necessary. If serving cold, cool, then chill and check the seasoning before serving.

3 Pour the watercress soup into bowls and top each portion with a spoonful of soft goat's cheese. Serve at once.

Jerusalem artichoke and rosemary soup

The Jerusalem artichoke may not be the most attractive looking vegetable, but it is has a lovely nutty, earthy flavour and makes an excellent smooth soup. Peeling the knobbly tubers can test your patience, but it is well worth the effort. When it comes to puréeing soups, I strongly recommend you use a proper blender or hand-held stick blender rather than a food processor, which won't produce a comparable velvety texture.

SERVES 4–6

good knob of butter
1 small onion, peeled and roughly chopped
1 small leek, trimmed, roughly chopped
  and rinsed
few rosemary sprigs
500g (1lb 2oz) Jerusalem artichokes, peeled
750ml (1¼ pints) vegetable stock
750ml (1¼ pints) milk
2 tablespoons double cream
sea salt and freshly ground white pepper

1   Melt the butter in a saucepan, add the onion, leek and rosemary sprigs, and cook gently for about 10 minutes until the vegetables are soft. Add the Jerusalem artichokes, most of the vegetable stock and the milk, and lightly season with salt and pepper. Bring to the boil, lower the heat and simmer for about 25 minutes, until the artichokes are tender.

2   Whiz the soup in a blender or using a hand-held blender until smooth, adding the reserved stock if necessary, to adjust the consistency. Pass through a fine-meshed sieve into a clean pan.

3   Add the cream to the soup and reheat gently to just below the boil, stirring. Adjust the seasoning if necessary before serving.

stocks

Stocks are at the heart of the professional kitchen, and a well flavoured stock will make all the difference – to soups and sauces in particular. But, of course, it's not absolutely essential to make your own, now that you can buy good quality stock cubes and powders, and even tubs of fresh stock.

When you make your own stock, do so in quantity, then boil the stock down to concentrate it and freeze in convenient amounts. Raw bones always make a better stock than leftover cooked ones, so ask your butcher to keep some fresh bones for you – they'll need to be chopped up.

Cooking time will depend on the type of stock you are making. Don't overcook it or the stock will lose its freshness and may have a bitter taste. Fresh vegetables are essential too. Peel your onions for a light coloured stock or leave the skins on to darken the colour. Lastly, don't add salt to your stock, as you may want to reduce it down later.

▲ **vegetable stock**
To make 1–1½ litres (1¾–2½ pints), roughly chop 3 onions, 3 garlic cloves, 1 small head of celery, 3 leeks (rinse well) and 5 carrots, then place in a large saucepan with 2 bay leaves, a few thyme sprigs, 20 black peppercorns, a small bunch of parsley and 1 tsp fennel seeds. Cover with cold water, bring to the boil, skim and simmer for 30–40 minutes. Strain through a fine sieve. Taste and if the flavour isn't strong enough, boil to reduce the stock down.

chicken stock

To make 1–1½ litres (1¾–2½ pints): rinse and chop 2kg (4½lb) chicken bones. Roughly chop 3 leeks (rinse well), 3 onions and 3 celery stalks. Put in a large pan with the bones, 1 bay leaf, few thyme sprigs, 2 chopped garlic cloves and 10 black peppercorns. Cover with cold water, bring to a boil and skim. Simmer for 2 hours, topping up with water and skimming as necessary. Strain through a fine sieve and skim. Boil to concentrate if necessary.

▼ dark meat stock

To make 1–1½ litres (1¾–2½ pints), you need 2kg (4½lb) chopped beef, veal, lamb or chicken bones, or a mixture. Roughly chop 3 onions, 5 carrots, a few celery stalks, 2 leeks (rinse well) and ½ head of garlic. Put in a roasting tin with the bones and roast at 200°C, gas 6 for about 15–20 minutes until golden brown, stirring every so often. Stir in 1½ tbsp tomato purée and roast for another 10 minutes. Tip the bones

fish stock

To make 1–1½ litres (1¾–2½ pints), rinse 2kg (4½lb) white fish bones (sole, brill, etc) and put in a large pan. Chop 2 leeks (rinse well), 2 onions and ½ head celery. Add to the pan with ½ lemon, 1 tsp fennel seeds, 20 black peppercorns, 1 bay leaf, a few thyme sprigs and a handful of parsley. Cover with cold water and bring to a boil; skim. Simmer gently for 20 minutes, skimming occasionally. Strain through a fine sieve. Taste the stock and boil to reduce if the flavour isn't strong enough.

and vegetables into a large saucepan, cover with cold water and add 10 black peppercorns, a few thyme sprigs and 1 bay leaf. Bring to the boil, skim and simmer for 3–4 hours, topping up with water as necessary to keep the ingredients covered and skimming occasionally. Strain through a fine sieve and skim off any fat. Check the flavour and boil to reduce it if it isn't strong enough. If making a sauce, reduce the stock until starting to thicken and add a little cornflour mixed with water to achieve the consistency required.

Cullen skink

Cullen is the village on the coast of the Moray Firth where this classic Scottish soup originated, and 'skink' is an ancient word for a broth or soup. This is substantial enough to be served as a main course or brunch dish. Avoid the yellow-dyed smoked haddock and buy the lighter coloured natural smoked fillets or Arbroath smokies, which are on the bone.

SERVES 4–6

1 leek, trimmed

good knob of butter

1.2 litres (2 pints) fish stock

1 floury potato, about 200g (7oz), peeled and
   roughly chopped

1 bay leaf

300g (11oz) undyed smoked haddock fillets

4 tablespoons double cream

1 tablespoon chopped parsley

sea salt and freshly ground white pepper

1 Roughly chop the leek and rinse thoroughly in cold water, then drain and pat dry. Melt the butter in a pan, stir in the leek, cover and cook gently for a few minutes until soft.

2 Add the fish stock, potato, bay leaf and smoked haddock. Bring to a simmer, season and cook gently for 15 minutes. With a slotted spoon, carefully remove the smoked haddock from the pan to a plate and put to one side. Simmer the soup for a further 15 minutes.

3 Remove the bay leaf and whiz the soup in a blender or using a hand-held blender until smooth. Pass through a fine-meshed sieve into a clean pan.

4 Skin and flake the smoked haddock, checking for any bones. Stir the cream and parsley into the soup and bring back to a simmer. Add the flaked haddock and adjust the seasoning, if necessary. Heat through gently, then serve.

Cornish red mullet soup

Cornish red mullet has a delicious taste of the sea. Plainly fried, the fillets make a lovely main course, and you can use the bones for the soup. Fresh mullet is preferable, but you can use frozen ones here. British red mullet is seasonal and can be hard to find, but you could use sea bream, sea bass or gurnard, or even a mixture of fish. The soup freezes well, so consider making a double batch when you're lucky enough to come across fresh red mullet.

SERVES 4–6

2 tablespoons olive oil

500g (1lb 2oz) whole red mullet, cleaned
   and roughly chopped

1 small onion, peeled and roughly chopped

1/2 leek, trimmed, roughly chopped and rinsed

1/2 small fennel bulb, roughly chopped

1/2 red pepper, deseeded and roughly chopped

1 small potato, about 125g (4oz), peeled and
   roughly chopped

3 garlic cloves, peeled and chopped

good pinch of saffron threads

5 black peppercorns

2 juniper berries

1 bay leaf

few thyme sprigs

3 tablespoons tomato purée

150g canned chopped tomatoes

150ml (1/4 pint) red wine

1.5 litres (2 1/2 pints) fish stock

sea salt and freshly ground black or
   white pepper

1   Heat the olive oil in a large heavy-based pan and gently fry the chopped red mullet, vegetables, garlic, spices and herbs for about 10 minutes. Add the tomato purée, chopped tomatoes, red wine and fish stock. Bring to the boil, season with salt and pepper, and simmer for 50 minutes.

2   Blend about one third of the soup (bones and all) in a blender, or using a hand-held blender, until smooth. Return to the rest of the soup in the pot and simmer gently for another 20 minutes.

3   Strain the soup by pushing it through a medium-meshed sieve or conical strainer with the back of a ladle into a clean pan. Reheat gently and adjust the seasoning to serve.

leek and oyster soup

Those of you who are squeamish about oysters might like to try this soup as an introduction to these little gems of the sea. The flavour of the ocean is still present, but they are no longer alive.

SERVES 4

good knob of butter
3 medium leeks, trimmed, roughly chopped
  and rinsed
750ml (1¼ pints) fish stock
8 oysters, opened (see page 36), juices saved
2 tablespoons double cream
1 tablespoon finely chopped chives
sea salt and freshly ground white pepper

1 Melt the butter in a pan, add the leeks, cover and cook gently until soft, without allowing them to colour. Add the fish stock, bring to the boil, season with salt and pepper and simmer for 10 minutes.

2 Remove the soup from the heat, add half of the oysters and the cream, and whiz until smooth in a blender or using a hand-held blender.

3 Pass the soup through a fine-meshed sieve into a clean pan and season again, if necessary. Bring back to a simmer, then remove from the heat and add the remaining oysters and the chives.

4 Serve in warm shallow soup bowls or pasta bowls, spooning an oyster into each one.

crab soup

This soup acquires its flavour from the shells, so you can use most of the meat from the crab for a salad or sandwich. If you can't get whole crabs, use cooked or raw prawns in shells with heads.

SERVES 4–6

1kg (2¼lb) prepared whole crab (see page 42)
1 tablespoon vegetable oil
1 small onion, peeled and roughly chopped
1 small leek, trimmed, chopped and rinsed
3 garlic cloves, peeled and roughly chopped
½ teaspoon fennel seeds
few thyme sprigs

1 bay leaf
40g (1½oz) butter
2 tablespoons tomato purée
3 tablespoons flour
1 glass of dry white wine
1.5 litres (2½ pints) fish stock
100ml (3½fl oz) double cream
sea salt and freshly ground white pepper

1 Set the crabmeat to one side. With a heavy chopping knife or cleaver, break the body and leg shells up into small pieces. Heat the oil in a large heavy-based saucepan and fry the crab shells over a high heat for about 5 minutes, stirring every so often until they begin to colour.

2 Add the onion, leek, garlic, fennel seeds, thyme and bay leaf, and cook for another 5 minutes or until the vegetables begin to colour. Add the butter and melt, then add the tomato purée and flour, stir well and cook gently for a minute or so. Add the wine, then slowly stir in the fish stock. Bring to the boil, lower the heat, season and simmer for 1 hour.

3 Strain the soup through a colander over a bowl. Discard the hard claws and main shell, retaining about a third of the softer white body shells in the colander. Add these to the strained liquid and whiz in a blender or strong food processor, then strain through a fine-meshed sieve into a clean pan.

4 Bring the soup to a simmer, then stir in the cream and crabmeat. Warm through gently, check the seasoning and serve in warm bowls.

Scotch broth

This hearty, comforting, stew-like soup is ideal served as a warming main course on a cold winter's day, with some crusty bread. It is also one of those dishes that almost tastes better the day after it's made. You will need to remember to soak the split peas overnight.

SERVES 4–6

50g (2oz) dried green or yellow split peas
25g (1oz) pearl barley
200g (7oz) neck of lamb fillet
1/2 teaspoon chopped thyme leaves
2 litres (31/2 pints) lamb or chicken stock
1 small leek, trimmed, slit lengthways
  and rinsed
2 carrots, peeled
1 celery stalk, strings removed if necessary
1 small turnip, peeled
few leaves of green cabbage, stalks removed
1 tablespoon chopped parsley
sea salt and freshly ground black pepper

1 Soak the split peas in cold water to cover overnight, then drain and rinse. Soak the pearl barley in a separate bowl of cold water for 1 hour, then drain.

2 Cut the lamb roughly into 1cm (1/2 inch) cubes and place in a large heavy-based pan with the thyme, barley and split peas. Cover with the stock and season with a little salt and pepper, bring to the boil and simmer for 1 hour, skimming from time to time.

3 Meanwhile, cut the leek, carrots, celery, turnip and cabbage roughly into 1cm (1/2 inch) dice. Add the vegetables, except the cabbage, to the pan and simmer for another 30 minutes.

4 Add the cabbage and parsley to the soup and simmer for a further 10 minutes. Skim any fat from the surface, check the seasoning and serve.

brown Windsor soup

This traditional soup is distinctly out of favour these days and rarely seen on menus, but in the right hands, it can be a delicious winter warmer. You could easily cheat and blend any braise, such as beef or oxtail, with a little cream sherry – probably how the soup came about in the first instance – but don't try to purée the Sunday roast and gravy. Here's how to make it from scratch.

SERVES 4–6

300g (11oz) braising steak
2–3 tablespoons vegetable oil
1 onion, peeled and roughly chopped
1 small carrot, peeled and roughly chopped
1 small leek, trimmed, roughly chopped
  and rinsed
good knob of butter
2 tablespoons plain flour
1 teaspoon tomato purée
1 garlic clove, peeled and crushed
few thyme sprigs
1 small bay leaf
3 litres (5 pints) beef stock
2 tablespoons cream sherry
sea salt and freshly ground black pepper

1 Cut the braising steak into bite-sized pieces. Heat the oil in a large heavy-based saucepan and fry the meat and vegetables, stirring over a high heat until nicely browned.

2 Add the butter to the pan and stir, then add the flour and cook, stirring, for another couple of minutes. Add the tomato purée, garlic, thyme and bay leaf, then gradually add the beef stock, stirring well to avoid lumps. Bring to a simmer, season with salt and pepper, and simmer for 2 hours, until the meat is tender.

3 Whiz the soup in a blender or using a hand-held blender until smooth, then strain through a sieve into a clean pan. The soup should be rich in flavour and a nice brown colour; if not, simmer for a little longer to concentrate the flavour.

4 Adjust the seasoning if necessary, and stir the sherry into the soup just before serving.

London particular

This thick, warming soup was given its name by Charles Dickens, referring to the fog that once formed a blanket around London, a 'pea souper'. It is an ideal way to use the stock from boiled ham (page 112) and some of the leftover meat. Depending on the ham, the stock can be quite salty, so taste it before starting to make the soup and dilute with water if necessary. Remember to soak the split peas overnight, or buy 'quick-soak' peas that don't require lengthy soaking.

SERVES 4–6
250g (9oz) dried green split peas
25g (1oz) butter
1 onion, peeled and roughly chopped
few thyme sprigs
1–1.5 litres (1¾–2½ pints) ham stock, plus about
   150g (5oz) leftover ham (see page 112)
freshly ground black pepper (and salt
   if necessary)

1   Soak the dried split peas in cold water to cover overnight or according to the packet instructions.

2   Drain the split peas. Melt the butter in a heavy-based saucepan, add the onion and cook gently for 5 minutes or so until soft, without allowing it to colour. Add the thyme sprigs, split peas and 1 litre (1¾ pints) of the ham stock. Bring to the boil and skim, then add some pepper (but no salt).

3   Simmer for 1 hour or until the peas are cooked, topping up with more stock or water as necessary. The cooking time will depend on the age of the peas. They should be cooked until they are soft and beginning to fall apart.

4   Whiz the soup in a blender or using a hand-held blender to the desired texture – make it as coarse or as smooth as you like and add a little water if it is too thick. (If the soup is too thin, you can simmer it for a little longer to reduce and thicken.) Check the seasoning and add a little salt and more pepper if necessary.

5   Shred the cooked ham trimmings and add to the soup. Reheat in the pan and simmer for a few more minutes before serving.

2 starters, snacks and savouries

minted summer vegetable salad with goat's cheese

Salad leaves have certainly moved on since the days of the floppy English round lettuce. Forgotten varieties of leaf have been revived and vegetable leaves like spinach and chard are harvested in their juvenile stage for the salad bowl. In response to customer demand, supermarket shelves now offer a wide range of quality salad leaves, often ready washed and mixed. Here young leaves are combined with the pick of early summer vegetables – broad beans, peas and asparagus.

SERVES 4

65g (2¹/₂oz) shelled fresh or frozen peas
100g (3¹/₂oz) podded fresh young broad beans
100g (3¹/₂oz) asparagus tips
65g (2¹/₂oz) small salad leaves (1 or 2 varieties)
small mint leaves, from 2 or 3 sprigs
75g (3oz) soft goat's cheese, broken into
   small pieces
small handful of fine chives, trimmed

FOR THE DRESSING:

1 tablespoon good quality white wine vinegar
   (preferably Chardonnay)
3 tablespoons olive oil
2 tablespoons vegetable or corn oil
1 teaspoon caster sugar
few mint leaves
sea salt and freshly ground black pepper

1 Cook the vegetables separately in boiling salted water until just tender; allow 5–7 minutes for peas, 3–4 minutes for broad beans, 2–3 minutes for asparagus.

2 Meanwhile, make the dressing. Whiz the wine vinegar, oils, sugar and mint leaves together in a blender or food processor and season with salt and pepper to taste.

3 Drain the vegetables, refresh briefly in cold water to stop the cooking and drain again. (If the broad beans aren't as small and young as they might be, slip them out of their skins after cooking.) Toss the warm drained vegetables with a spoonful or two of the dressing and season with salt and pepper.

4 Combine the salad leaves and mint leaves in a bowl and lightly dress with some of the dressing. Divide between serving plates, scatter the vegetables on top and spoon over a little more dressing. Arrange the pieces of goat's cheese on top and finish with the chives.

oysters with shallot vinegar

Oysters are a part of English history. The Romans loved our Colchester oysters so much they designated the town, Camulodunum as it was then called, the capital of Roman England. Except for oyster enthusiasts who tend to take them for granted, most of us miss out on their pure taste of the sea. Our native season officially starts in September and lasts through the following months with an 'r'. However, October is generally held to be the best time to start eating them.

Opening or 'shucking' oysters can be a daunting experience. If you haven't tackled it before, I suggest you buy an oyster knife with a guard to protect your hand.

SERVES 4

24 oysters

seaweed and/or crushed ice, to serve

FOR THE SHALLOT VINEGAR:

4 shallots, peeled and very finely diced

100ml (3½fl oz) good quality red wine vinegar

 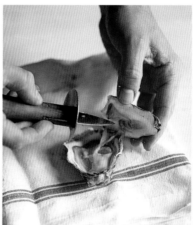 

1 First make the shallot vinegar. Mix the shallots and red wine vinegar together in a bowl and set aside to infuse for 1 hour.

2 Now prise open the oysters. Lay an oyster in a folded tea towel on a surface with the flat shell uppermost and the pointed hinge facing towards you. Holding the oyster down with the cloth, force the tip of the oyster knife into the hinge of the shell, carefully moving it from side to side until you can feel the shell loosening – it will take some force.

3 Keep the knife in the shell, twisting it a little and run it along the top of the flat shell until you feel the muscle, which attaches the oyster to the shell. Cut through this to detach the top shell.

4 Remove any bits of shell that may be on the oyster flesh, but don't pour away the natural juices. You can loosen the oyster meat from the curved shell for your guests and flip it over or let them do it themselves. Line four plates with seaweed and/or crushed ice and place a small bowl of shallot vinegar in the centre. Arrange 6 oysters on each plate and serve.

deep-fried whitebait

Whitebait are the small fry of herrings and sprats. Deep-fried whitebait are now a familiar starter in restaurants all over the country, though they were considered a delicacy before the arrival of frozen food. Whitebait dinners were first held at Dagenham to celebrate the completion of the vast land-draining scheme in Essex. I find these fish are best cooked from frozen; shake them in a dry tea towel to lose excess ice glaze before coating and deep-frying.

SERVES 4

300g (11oz) frozen whitebait
vegetable or corn oil, for deep-frying
4 tablespoons plain flour
1 teaspoon sea salt, plus extra to sprinkle
good pinch of cayenne pepper
125ml (4fl oz) milk
lemon wedges, to serve

1 Preheat the oven to low, 110°C (fan oven 100°C), gas mark ¼, to keep the whitebait warm once you have deep-fried them. Heat an 8–9cm (3½ inch) depth of oil in a deep-fat fryer or heavy-based deep saucepan to 175–180°C.

2 Mix the flour, salt and cayenne pepper together in one bowl. Pour the milk into another. The next stage is a bit of a messy job. While the whitebait are still frozen, toss them first in the flour to coat, shake off any excess and put them into the milk. Drain them from the milk, shaking off any excess and then drop them back into the flour. Once again, shake off any excess flour and put them on a plate or tray ready to fry.

3 Cook the whitebait in two or three batches, depending on the size of your deep-fryer or pan, for 2–3 minutes each, stirring occasionally with a slotted spoon so they don't stick together. Remove with the slotted spoon and drain on kitchen paper. Keep warm in the low oven while you cook the rest.

4 Divide the deep-fried whitebait between warm plates and sprinkle with a little salt. Serve at once, with lemon wedges.

soused mackerel

This is an old way of preserving your catch, and the end result (which will keep for up to a week in the fridge) is delicious with brown bread and butter for supper. Mackerel are scavengers and will take their own flesh for bait, which is what we used as kids when fishing. Within a day or so of being caught, they are delicious grilled or pan-fried. After that, however, because of their oily flesh, they become a little bitter tasting, hence the sousing.

My grandmother always used malt vinegar as, in those days, white wine vinegar had not yet made it to the West Country. I wasn't the slightest bit interested in cooking then, but I think this is more or less the recipe she used.

SERVES 4

8 mackerel fillets, each about 80–100g
(3–3¹/₂oz), trimmed
2 small onions, peeled and cut into thin rings
1 carrot, peeled and thinly sliced on the
diagonal
1 bay leaf
8 peppercorns
¹/₂ teaspoon sea salt
¹/₂ teaspoon fennel seeds
125ml (4fl oz) white wine vinegar

1 Preheat the oven to 180°C (fan oven 160°C), gas mark 4. Check over the mackerel fillets and remove any small pin bones with tweezers. Roll up the fillets, skin-side out, and secure each with a cocktail stick. Put into an ovenproof dish, not too close together.

2 Put all the rest of the ingredients into a saucepan with 90ml (3fl oz) water and bring to the boil.

3 Pour the vinegar mixture over the mackerel fillets, cover the dish with a lid or foil and cook in the oven for 25 minutes. Leave to cool in the dish.

4 Serve the soused mackerel with brown bread and butter.

potted salmon with pickled cucumber

Potting is an old-fashioned way of preserving. This potted salmon makes a good all-year-round starter or snack, or can even be used as a sandwich filling (open or closed). The pickled cucumber helps to cut the richness of the butter, and it can be served with other foods, from cheese to poached fish to cold meats. You will need to prepare the pickled cucumbers well ahead.

SERVES 4–6

325g (11oz) salmon fillet, skinned
75g (3oz) smoked salmon, finely chopped
125g (4oz) unsalted butter, softened
1 tablespoon thick yogurt
1/2 tablespoon finely chopped chives
juice of 1/2 lemon
sea salt
good pinch of cayenne pepper

FOR THE PICKLED CUCUMBER:

1 medium cucumber
200ml (7fl oz) white wine vinegar
2 large shallots, peeled and thinly sliced
1 teaspoon mustard seeds
4 teaspoons caster sugar
sea salt and coarsely ground black pepper
1 tablespoon finely chopped dill
a little olive oil, to taste

1 First prepare the pickled cucumber. Halve the cucumber lengthways, scoop out the seeds, then slice thinly at an angle and put into a bowl. Meanwhile, put the vinegar, shallots, mustard seeds, sugar, salt and pepper into a pan and bring to the boil, then remove from the heat and leave to cool a little. Pour over the cucumbers and set aside for an hour, stirring every so often. Mix in the dill. Transfer to a sterilised Kilner jar, seal and store in a cool dark place, or keep in a covered bowl in the fridge if using within a few days.

2 Check over the salmon and remove any small pin bones with tweezers. Put the salmon into a saucepan, just cover with cold water and add 1 teaspoon salt. Bring to the boil, lower the heat and simmer for 2 minutes. Remove from the heat and leave the fish to cool in the liquid; it will finish cooking in the residual heat.

3 Drain the cooled salmon and flake the flesh into a bowl. In another bowl, carefully mix the smoked salmon and softened butter. Add the yogurt, chives and lemon juice, season with salt and cayenne pepper, and mix well. Fold in the flaked salmon, being careful not to break the pieces up too much.

4 Before serving, drain off the liquid from the pickled cucumber (you can save it for another batch). Toss the drained cucumbers with a little olive oil.

5 Serve the potted salmon at room temperature, not refrigerator-cold, either naturally spooned on to a plate or in little ramekins, with hot toast and the pickled cucumbers.

dressed crab

You can't beat freshly cooked crab, accompanied by some good mayonnaise and brown bread and butter. I prefer to tackle the thing whole myself (perhaps because I was brought up by the seaside), armed with crackers and a finger bowl and a glass of white wine. If you prefer the 'no bones and mess' approach, you can buy ready-picked white and brown meat, although it generally doesn't have quite the same taste unless your fishmonger does it for you.

The white meat has a superb taste and texture. The brown meat, however, can be a little dry and may need spicing up a bit – simply adding breadcrumbs just doesn't do it for me. Try the recipe for brown crab mayonnaise below – it transforms the brown meat into something else. If you chose to serve the crabmeat out of the shell, allow 100g (3½oz) as a starter or 150g (5oz) per person as a main course. The weight of the brown meat can be unpredictable, so you could buy some more ready-picked to be sure you have enough.

It isn't difficult to prepare a fresh crab yourself. Follow the instructions on the opposite page; each of the technique photographs in the sequence below relates to a preparation step.

SERVES 4

2 cooked crabs, each about 1kg (2¼lb)

TO SERVE:
lemon wedges
brown bread and butter

FOR THE BROWN CRAB MAYONNAISE (OPTIONAL):
juice of ½ lemon, or to taste
2 teaspoons tomato ketchup
1 teaspoon Worcestershire sauce
1 teaspoon English mustard
65–75g (2½–3oz) brown bread,
   crusts removed and broken into small pieces
2–3 tablespoons good quality
   mayonnaise
sea salt and freshly ground white pepper

1 First you need to get the meat out of the crab. Lay the crab on its back and twist off the claws.

2 Crack the claws open with a mallet or rolling pin and remove the white meat. Now turn the main body on its back and twist off the pointed flap.

3 Push the tip of a table knife between the main shell and the body section and twist the blade to separate the two, then push the body up and remove from the outer shell. Remove the dead man's fingers (the feather like, grey gills attached to the body) and discard.

4 Split the body section in half with a heavy knife and then split each half in two. Now you need to be patient and pick out the white meat from the little cavities in the body using a lobster pick or a teaspoon. Go through the white meat carefully to make sure there are no residual bits of shell.

5 Loosen the brown meat in the main shell with a teaspoon and scoop it out into a bowl. Check that there are no fragments of shell, then put to one side. Scrub the shell if you wish to serve the crab in it.

6 To prepare the main shell for serving, look for the natural line on the underside. Push the open edge gently with your fingers into the shell and it will break along the line, leaving a neat shell. Wash the shell under warm water and pat dry. Spoon the brown meat, or the brown crab mayonnaise, into the centre and the white meat on either side. Serve with lemon wedges and brown bread and butter.

brown crab mayonnaise Put the brown crab, lemon juice, ketchup, Worcestershire sauce and mustard into a blender or food processor and whiz until smooth. Add the bread and process again until smooth. Transfer to a bowl, whisk in the mayonnaise and season with salt and white pepper. Add a little more lemon juice, if necessary. Refrigerate for an hour or so before serving.

asparagus

English asparagus has a short season, starting in early May and lasting 6 weeks or so, depending on the weather, but imported asparagus is available year round. There are many different varieties on offer: thick green, medium green, thin sprue and white.

I've never owned an asparagus boiler – a tall pan with a basket, designed so the tougher stalks cook in the water while the tips steam gently. Sounds too complicated – a large saucepan works fine for me.

To prepare asparagus, cut or break off the woody ends. Thin asparagus (pencil thick) or very thin (sprue), doesn't need peeling. Thicker stalks should be peeled with a fine swivel vegetable peeler, starting about 5cm (2 inches) down from the tips. Cook in gently simmering, salted water until tender: 2 minutes for sprue, 4–5 minutes for finger-thick spears and a few minutes longer for thicker stems. Drain and serve with buttery hollandaise sauce or mayonnaise (see right).

▲ **boiled duck's egg with asparagus soldiers**
To serve 4, carefully place 4 duck eggs in a pan of boiling water and boil for 6 minutes for duck eggs (4–5 minutes for hens). Meanwhile, add 1kg (2¼lb) prepared medium to thick asparagus to a pan of boiling salted water and cook for about 5 minutes. Cut the tops from the eggs and put them into egg cups. Drain the asparagus and arrange in bundles next to the eggs, for dipping. Serve with a little pile of Maldon sea salt.

mayonnaise

To serve 4–6, whisk 2 medium egg yolks, 1 tsp English mustard, 2 tsp Dijon mustard and 2 tsp white wine vinegar in a bowl with salt and white pepper. Slowly trickle in 100ml (3½fl oz) olive oil mixed with 200ml (7fl oz) vegetable oil, whisking constantly. If it becomes too thick at any point, add a few drops of water and continue whisking in the oil. Adjust seasoning and add a little lemon juice. Store in a sealed jar in the fridge for up to 2 weeks.

▼ hollandaise sauce

To serve 4–6, put 3 tbsp white wine vinegar, 1 chopped small shallot, a few tarragon sprigs, 1 bay leaf, 5 black peppercorns and 3 tbsp water in a pan and boil to reduce to 2 tsp. Strain and cool. Melt 200g (7oz) unsalted butter in a small pan and simmer for 5 minutes. Cool a little, then pour off the clarified butter, leaving the sediment. Put 3 small egg yolks in a small bowl with half the reduced vinegar and whisk over a pan of

fried egg with sprue asparagus

To serve 4, melt a knob of butter in a small non-stick frying pan over a low heat. Crack in an egg, season the white with a little sea salt and cook gently until the white has just set. Do the same with 3 more eggs (using 2 pans if available); keep warm. Meanwhile cook 200g (7oz) trimmed sprue asparagus in boiling salted water for 2 minutes or until tender. Drain, return to the pan and toss with 50–75g (2–3oz) good quality salted butter. Scatter on top of the eggs, season and serve.

gently simmering water until it begins to thicken and become frothy. Slowly trickle in the butter, whisking constantly; if added too quickly the sauce will separate. When you've added two thirds, add some or all of the remaining vinegar reduction to taste. Then add the rest of the butter. The vinegar should just cut the oiliness of the butter. Season with salt and white pepper, cover with cling film and leave in a warm, not hot, place until needed. The hollandaise sauce can be reheated over a bowl of hot water and lightly whisked again to serve.

chicken livers with wild mushrooms

Wild mushrooms are increasingly available in shops and supermarkets these days, and more and more people are picking their own. Obviously you should only do so if you can differentiate between edible and non-edible varieties with total confidence. Unless it is really necessary to wash them, just trim and brush or wipe the mushrooms to clean them. There are many less common cultivated mushrooms on supermarket shelves as well nowadays, but shiitake are best reserved for oriental dishes in my view. If wild mushrooms are unavailable, oyster mushrooms are probably the best alternative.

Illustrated on previous page

SERVES 4

300g (11oz) fresh chicken livers, halved if large
2–3 tablespoons vegetable oil
300g (11oz) wild mushrooms, cleaned and
  halved or quartered if large
2 garlic cloves, crushed
100g (3½oz) butter
2 tablespoons chopped parsley
sea salt and freshly ground black pepper

1 Check over the chicken livers and remove any white sinews. Also look out for, and remove any green bile sac, which can leave a rather nasty taste in the mouth. Pat the chicken livers dry on some kitchen paper and season lightly with salt and pepper.

2 Heat 1 tablespoon oil in a heavy-based frying pan until just beginning to smoke and quickly fry the livers for a minute on each side, until nicely coloured but still pink inside, then transfer them to a plate.

3 Clean the pan, add a little oil and heat it again. Add the mushrooms and garlic, season with salt and pepper and fry over a high heat for a few minutes, stirring occasionally until they begin to soften and are lightly coloured.

4 Return the livers to the pan with the mushrooms and add the butter. Cook for another minute or two, then add the parsley and stir well. Ideally the chicken livers should still be just a little pink inside. Spoon on to warm plates and serve straightaway.

angels on horseback

You may well have heard of 'devils on horseback', where prunes are the 'devil' wrapped in bacon. Here, oysters take the place of prunes as the 'angel' and they are served on toast. Sadly, savouries such as these are rarely seen outside of gentlemen's clubs, other than as hors d'oeuvre or party snacks. At one time they would have been one of the courses at a grand banquet, or served in a grand restaurant or at a formal dinner party before, after or instead of dessert.

SERVES 4

4 rashers of rindless streaky bacon, cut as thinly
  as possible
8 large oysters, removed from the shell
  (see page 36)
1 tablespoon vegetable oil
65g (2¹/₂oz) butter
2 shallots, peeled and finely diced
1 tablespoon chopped parsley
4 slices of baguette, cut at an angle, each
  1cm (¹/₂ inch) thick

1   Cut the bacon rashers across in half and, with the back of a knife on a chopping board, stretch the bacon as thinly as it will go, until almost translucent. Pat the oysters dry with some kitchen paper and wrap each one securely in a piece of bacon.

2   Heat a little oil in a heavy-based frying pan and quickly fry the wrapped oysters over a high heat for a minute or so on each side. Remove the bacon-wrapped oysters from the pan and set aside.

3   Melt the butter in the pan and add the shallots. Fry over a low heat for a minute or so, without allowing them to colour, then add the parsley and remove from the heat.

4   Meanwhile toast the bread on both sides, arrange 2 wrapped oysters on each slice and spoon the shallots and parsley over to serve.

jellied ham with piccalilli

This is a great way to use some of a home-cooked ham joint. Make the piccalilli at least a week ahead, and soak the ham overnight before cooking as it can sometimes be salty.

SERVES 6–8

1 ham hock, about 1kg (2¼lb), or a 700g (1½lb) ham joint, soaked overnight in plenty of cold water
few thyme sprigs
1 bay leaf
2 onions, peeled and quartered
3 celery stalks
10 black peppercorns
3–4 sheets of leaf gelatine (the smaller quantity if using a hock)
2 tablespoons chopped parsley

FOR THE PICCALILLI:

1 medium cucumber, halved and deseeded
½ large cauliflower, cut into small florets
1 onion, peeled and chopped
1 tablespoon salt
150g (5oz) caster sugar
65g (2½oz) English mustard
½ teaspoon ground turmeric
1 small chilli, deseeded and finely chopped
150ml (¼ pint) malt vinegar
125ml (4fl oz) white wine vinegar
1 tablespoon cornflour

1 First make the piccalilli. Cut the cucumber into 1cm (½ inch) pieces. Halve the cauliflower florets and place in a dish with the cucumber and onion. Sprinkle with the salt and leave for 1 hour. Rinse well, drain and put into a bowl. Put the sugar, mustard, turmeric, chilli and vinegars into a saucepan. Dissolve over a low heat, then simmer for 2–3 minutes. Mix the cornflour with 150ml (¼ pint) water and whisk into the vinegar mixture. Simmer gently, stirring, for 5 minutes. Pour the hot liquid over the vegetables and let cool. Pour into sterilised jars and refrigerate for at least a week before use, or up to 6 months.

2 Put the ham into a large saucepan with the thyme, bay leaf, onions, celery and peppercorns. Add water to cover, bring to the boil and simmer until the ham is tender, about 2 hours depending on the cut and size (refer to pack guidelines if applicable). Remove the ham from the liquid and leave to cool.

3 Skim the cooking liquor, measure 350ml (12fl oz) and bring to the boil in a pan. Meanwhile, soak the gelatine in cold water for few minutes to soften, then squeeze out excess water. Remove the liquor from the heat and add the gelatine, with the parsley, stirring to dissolve. Leave until cool, but not set.

4 Meanwhile, cut the ham into rough 1cm (½ inch) cubes, removing any fat, and put it into a bowl. Mix in a little of the cooled jellied liquor and pack into a 1.2 litre (2 pint) terrine. Top up with the remaining liquor (you may not need all of it). Cover with cling film and leave to set in the fridge overnight.

5 To serve, briefly dip the terrine into a bowl of boiling water and invert on to a chopping board to turn out. With a carving knife, cut it into 2cm (¾ inch) thick slices. Serve on individual plates, with the piccalilli.

omelette Arnold Bennett

Created at the Savoy Hotel for the writer and critic whose name it bears, this rich concoction seems to have disappeared from restaurant menus. To tell the truth, a busy kitchen stops dead when a couple of these are ordered, so that's probably why! It can be served as a main course or for brunch. If you haven't got small pans, then make one larger omelette in a non-stick frying pan and cut into four before glazing.

SERVES 4

200g (7oz) undyed smoked haddock fillet, skinned
1 shallot, peeled and finely chopped
150ml (¼ pint) double cream

8 large eggs, plus 1 extra egg yolk
1 tablespoon chopped parsley
good knob of butter
sea salt and freshly ground white pepper

1 Place the smoked haddock in a pan with the shallot and just cover with water. Bring to a simmer, cover with a lid and poach gently for 2 minutes. Remove with a slotted spoon and drain on kitchen paper. Continue to simmer the cooking liquid until it has almost completely reduced, then add the cream, and simmer to reduce by two thirds until thickened. Leave to cool a little.

2 Flake the smoked haddock, checking for any bones as you do so. Add the fish to the sauce with the egg yolk and parsley, stir well and season with salt and white pepper. Preheat the grill to high.

3 Heat a little butter in a small non-stick omelette or blini pan over a low heat. Beat the eggs in a bowl and season. Pour a quarter of the egg mixture into the pan and stir over a low heat with a wooden spatula, until beginning to set but still soft. Stop stirring.

4 Take a plate a little larger than the pan, place upside down on top of the pan and invert the omelette on to the plate. Transfer to a grill-proof plate or serving dish. Repeat with remaining mixture to make 4 small omelettes. Spoon the haddock mixture on top of the omelettes, spreading it evenly to cover. Put under the grill for a minute or two until evenly browned, then serve (minding the hot plates).

soft roes on toast

Herring roes, soft roes or milts, are normally sold frozen or defrosted, but are sometimes available fresh during the spring and early summer. Treat frozen ones correctly and no one will know the difference.

SERVES 4
450–500g (about 1lb) herring soft roes
150g (5oz) butter
flour, to dust
4 slices of bread (cut from a small bloomer)
65g (2¹/₂oz) drained capers
1 tablespoon chopped parsley
sea salt and freshly ground black pepper

1   Pat the roes dry on kitchen paper. Heat a knob of butter in a large (or 2 smaller) non-stick frying pan(s). Season the roes and flour lightly, shaking off excess. Add to the pan and cook over a medium heat on both sides until the roes turn golden brown and curl up.

2   Meanwhile, toast the bread on both sides. Pile the cooked roes on the toast. Melt the rest of the butter in the pan, add the capers and parsley, then spoon over the roes and serve.

Scotch woodcock

This is yet another savoury rarely seen on menus these days. It's good eaten as a light teatime snack or even for brunch. A few of the anchovies can be mashed and folded into the eggs once they are cooked for a more savoury flavour.

SERVES 4
25g (1oz) butter, plus extra to spread
4 eggs, beaten
1 tablespoon double cream
4 slices of bread (cut from a small bloomer)
sea salt and freshly ground black pepper

TO SERVE:
10 anchovy fillets in oil, drained and cut in half lengthways
10–12 large capers, drained and washed

1   Melt the butter in a heavy-based pan, add the eggs and cream with seasoning, and stir with a wooden spoon over a medium heat. The eggs should be nice and creamy when they are cooked.

2   Meanwhile, toast the bread on both sides and butter it. Spoon the eggs on to the toast and arrange the anchovies in a lattice on top. Scatter the capers over to serve.

Welsh rabbit

For years I thought it was 'rarebit'. I suppose you believe what you see on menus and never question it. After reading up on the subject, I was persuaded otherwise by various reputable food writers ... a Welsh joke maybe, once published and taken for granted. Anyway, refined cheese on toast with a few savoury additions is what it is.

SERVES 4

4 tablespoons Guinness
5 tablespoons double cream
150g (5oz) Cheddar cheese, grated
1 egg yolk
2 teaspoons Worcestershire sauce, or more
  to taste
1 teaspoon English mustard
8 thick slices of bread (cut from a small bloomer)
sea salt and freshly ground black pepper

1   Well in advance of serving, pour the Guinness into a small pan and simmer until reduced by half. Add the cream and simmer again until reduced by two thirds. Leave to cool.

2   Preheat a medium grill. Add the cheese, egg yolk, Worcestershire sauce and mustard to the reduced Guinness and season with salt and pepper to taste.

3   Toast the bread on both sides, then spread the cheese mixture on top, about 1cm (½ inch) thick, and to the edges to prevent these burning. Grill until the topping is nicely browned, then serve.

3 fish and seafood

Jerusalem artichoke and lobster salad with bacon

Don't be put off by the knobbly appearance of Jerusalem artichokes – once peeled or scraped and cooked, they have a delicious earthy flavour that goes with most meat or fish dishes. English Jerusalem artichokes are available from October through the winter months. Buy your lobsters cooked if you don't like the idea of dropping them into boiling water alive. Don't throw away the shells once you have prepared them, use them instead of crab to make the soup on page 27.

SERVES 4

500g (1lb 2oz) Jerusalem artichokes, peeled

2 lobsters, each about 500g (1lb 2oz), or one per person if you prefer

3 tablespoons good quality mayonnaise

1 tablespoon chopped chervil

8 thin rashers of rindless streaky bacon

sea salt and freshly ground white pepper

FOR THE DRESSING:

1 teaspoon tomato ketchup

2 teaspoons white wine vinegar

1 teaspoon Dijon mustard

3 tablespoons olive oil

1   Cook the artichokes in boiling salted water for 10–15 minutes, or until tender to the point of a knife. Drain them in a colander and return to the pan over a low heat for a minute or so, to drive off any excess water. Put them into a bowl and leave to cool.

2   Meanwhile, remove the head from the lobster and the main body shell by squeezing the shell in the palm of your hand until you feel it break, then carefully remove the meat intact by prising the shell open with your thumbs. Crack the claws with a mallet or rolling pin and extract the meat. Cut the lobster tail in half lengthways.

3   Preheat the grill. Mash the artichokes coarsely with a fork, then mix in the mayonnaise and three quarters of the chervil. Season with salt and pepper to taste.

4   Make the dressing by whisking all the ingredients together, seasoning with a little salt and freshly ground pepper.

5   Spoon the Jerusalem artichoke evenly into piles in the centres of four plates. Place a half lobster tail on top of each serving, with the claw meat. Grill the bacon until crisp and arrange on the lobster. Spoon the dressing around and sprinkle with the remaining chervil to serve.

herb baked queen scallops

When I was a kid, I remember seeing the trawlers struggling to make it into the harbour in Dorset's West Bay, piled high with 'queenies', as the queen scallops were known locally. They're quite small, about the size of a golf ball, and they are a bit tedious to prepare, but you can buy them shelled or in the half shell, ready cleaned. If you come across queen scallops in their shells, you'll find they are incredibly cheap. If you can't find queen scallops, 24 medium-sized ordinary scallops will do.

SERVES 4

32 queen scallops (in the half shell)

FOR THE HERB CRUST:
50g (2oz) butter
2 garlic cloves, peeled and crushed
1 tablespoon chopped parsley
40g (1¹/₂oz) fresh white breadcrumbs
sea salt and freshly ground black pepper

FOR THE GARLIC BUTTER:
100g (3¹/₂oz) butter
2 garlic cloves, peeled and crushed

1 To make the herb crust, melt the butter in a pan and gently cook the garlic for a minute without allowing it to colour. Stir in the parsley and breadcrumbs, and season with salt and pepper. Set aside.

2 Preheat the grill to high. Lay the scallops on a grill tray, scatter with the herb crust and cook under the hot grill for 3–4 minutes, until lightly coloured.

3 Meanwhile, make the garlic butter. Melt the butter in a pan until foaming, then add the garlic. Remove from the heat and spoon over the scallops to serve.

fish and chips

Abroad, we Brits are well known for our fish and chips. Strangely perhaps, this started off as regional food in the industrial north of England and, later, in the 19th century became popular in London's East End. The North has kept the tradition of simple fried fish and chips, with accompaniments like mushy peas and pickled onions and eggs.

Nowadays we are being urged to stay clear of cod and some other species from our waters, as over-fishing (and our 'play-safe' British palates) are depleting stocks. There are many other fish in the sea that we can cook, especially in batter. Fish that deep-fry well include cod, haddock, hake, sole, plaice and skate. Rock, also misleadingly called rock salmon, is a favourite at fish and chip shops. Known as dogfish or huss to fishermen, it is related to the shark.

Here is my take on traditional fish and chips, served with a minted pea purée. These quantities are sufficient for 4 people.

▲ **batter**
In a small bowl, dissolve 7g (¼oz) fast-action dried yeast in a little milk and leave in a warm place for about 10 minutes. Mix 250ml (8fl oz) milk, 1 small egg yolk, 75g (3oz) plain flour, 75g (3oz) cornflour, a pinch of cayenne and ¼ tsp baking powder to a batter and beat until smooth. Add the yeast mixture and season with salt. Cover and leave to stand for 1½–2 hours, until it begins to ferment. If the batter seems too thick, add a little more milk or water.

▼ fish

Heat a 10cm (4 inch) depth of vegetable oil in a deep-fat fryer or heavy-based saucepan to 175–180°C (or until a little batter dropped into the oil browns within 30 seconds). Buy 4 quality fish fillets, each 150–175g (5–6oz), remove any bones, then flour lightly. Dip in the batter, then fry in the hot oil, two at a time, until nicely browned, about 4–5 minutes. Drain and keep warm on a tray in a warm oven while you cook the rest.

▼ chips

Peel 800g–1kg (1¾ –2¼ lb) potatoes. For thick-cut chips, cut into 1cm (½ inch) slices, then into 1cm (½ inch) thick chips. For allumettes, cut 5mm (¼ inch) thick slices and sticks. Rinse in water and drain well on kitchen paper. Heat vegetable oil (or dripping or lard) to 120°C in a deep-fat fryer or heavy-based saucepan (no more than half full). Blanch your chips in the oil, 2 or 3 handfuls at a time, until soft but not coloured,

▲ minted pea purée

Heat 25g (1oz) butter in a pan, add 1 finely chopped large shallot and cook gently until soft. Add 400g (14oz) frozen peas, 100ml (3½fl oz) vegetable stock and 6–8 mint leaves. Season and simmer for 10–12 minutes. Blend in a food processor until smooth. Adjust the seasoning and set aside. Reheat the pea purée and stir in a knob of butter to serve.

then remove, drain and set aside. (You can store the chips like this in the fridge for up to a couple of days.)

To finish the chips, heat the oil to 175–180°C and re-fry them in the same way until crisp and golden. Season lightly with salt and serve immediately. You can keep early batches of cooked chips warm and crisp on an uncovered baking tray (in a single layer) in a warm oven. If your chips do go soggy, put the whole lot into a frying basket and dip them into the hot oil for a few seconds to warm and crisp them up again.

skate with shrimps and capers

Some people are put off skate because it is normally served 'on the bone', or rather on its cartilage framework. In fact, skate is very easy to eat because the flesh easily forks away from the 'bones'. If you are cooking several pieces, you may find it easier to brown them quickly on each side and finish cooking in the oven preheated to 200°C (fan oven 180°C), gas mark 6 for about 10 minutes.

SERVES 4

4 skate wings, each about 200–250g (7–9oz),
   skinned and trimmed
flour, to dust
1–2 tablespoons vegetable or corn oil
150g (5oz) unsalted butter

65g (2¹/₂oz) drained good quality capers, rinsed
juice of 1 lemon
75–90g (3–3¹/₂oz) cooked, peeled brown shrimps
   or prawns
1 tablespoon chopped parsley
sea salt and freshly ground white pepper

1   Season the skate wings and lightly flour them, shaking off excess. Heat the oil in a large heavy-based frying pan (preferably non-stick) and add the skate in a single layer. Cook for 3–5 minutes on each side until golden, adding about a third of the butter to the pan when they are almost cooked (to give them a nice brown colour). When the skate wings are done, remove from the pan and keep warm.

2   Wipe the pan out with some kitchen paper, add the rest of the butter and heat it gently until it begins to foam. Add the capers, lemon juice, shrimps or prawns and parsley, and remove from the heat.

3   Put the skate on warm plates and spoon the shrimp and caper butter evenly over the top. Serve with spinach and good buttery mash.

fillet of salmon with samphire

Samphire is available along our coastline during the summer months. It is delicious with simply cooked fish, as it has a naturally salty taste of the sea. In dishes like this I prefer to keep the skin on the salmon as it helps to retain some of the delicate juices during cooking. It can always be removed before serving if you prefer.

SERVES 4

65g (2½oz) butter
4 salmon fillets, each about 150–160g (5–5½oz),
  with skin (scales removed)
150g (5oz) samphire, washed and woody
  stalks removed
sea salt and freshly ground white pepper

1 Preheat the oven to 200°C (fan oven 180°C), gas mark 6 and rub a baking dish with a little of the butter. Meanwhile, check over the salmon and remove any small pin bones with tweezers.

2 Season the salmon fillets with salt and pepper and lay them in the prepared baking dish, skin facing up. Rub them with the rest of the butter, cover with foil and bake for 10 minutes.

3 Add the samphire and cook for a further 5 minutes. Spoon the samphire on to warm plates and place the salmon fillets on top. Drizzle over the cooking juices and serve.

poached salmon and asparagus salad

Despite what you may read in the papers, the quality of farmed salmon has improved immensely over the years. The price has also dropped, which makes it such a good value fish for the family. This is a simple, light summer dish, although with asparagus available most of the year now, it could be served as a light winter main course.

SERVES 4

600g (1¼lb) salmon fillet, skinned

150–200g (5–7oz) thin asparagus tips

75–100g (3–3½oz) small salad leaves, such as corn salad, oak leaf, baby spinach

10–12 chives, cut into short lengths

FOR THE POACHING LIQUID:

3 tablespoons olive oil

few thyme sprigs

1 bay leaf

1 teaspoon fennel seeds

½ glass of white wine

200ml (7fl oz) fish stock

sea salt and freshly ground white pepper

FOR THE DRESSING:

1 tablespoon good quality white wine vinegar (preferably Chardonnay)

1 teaspoon thin honey

1 teaspoon grainy mustard

4 tablespoons olive oil

1 teaspoon chopped chervil

1 teaspoon chopped chives

1 First prepare the poaching liquid. Put the olive oil, thyme, bay leaf, fennel seeds, white wine and fish stock into a wide, shallow saucepan. Season with salt and pepper, bring to the boil and simmer for 2–3 minutes.

2 Meanwhile, remove any small pin bones from the salmon with tweezers. Put the fish into the liquid and lay a piece of greaseproof paper directly on top of it. Simmer very gently for 3–4 minutes, then remove from the heat. Leave the salmon to cool in the liquid until required.

3 Bring a pan of salted water to the boil, add the asparagus tips and cook for 2–3 minutes until tender. Remove with a slotted spoon and leave on a plate to cool a little.

4 To make the dressing, whisk the wine vinegar with the honey and mustard. Gradually whisk in the olive oil and herbs, and season with salt and pepper.

5 Remove the salmon from the cooking liquid and pat dry with kitchen paper. Arrange the salad leaves on plates, then flake the salmon into pieces over the leaves. Arrange the asparagus on top, season lightly and spoon over the dressing. Scatter the chives on top.

grilled mackerel with gooseberry sauce

Mackerel are available through the summer months, but must be eaten as fresh as possible. I remember catching mackerel off the pier in Dorset's West Bay as a kid and taking them straight home to cook. They would curl up in the pan, due to rigor mortis because they were so fresh, but the taste was incredible – even to my inexperienced palate. That is one extreme and, unless you fish or know someone who does, you will never experience the taste. Two or three days is probably their maximum keeping time, until they begin to taste bitter.

Gooseberry sauce sounds like an odd thing to combine with the fish, but the two come into season at more or less the same time and the acidity of the gooseberries complements mackerel perfectly. Frozen gooseberries are available all year round and are very good in the sauce.

SERVES 4

4 whole mackerel, each about 200g (7oz),
  cleaned and heads removed
good knob of butter
250g (9oz) gooseberries, topped and tailed
2 teaspoons caster sugar
1/2 glass of white wine
150ml (1/4 pint) double cream
oil, to brush
sea salt and freshly ground white pepper

1 Make 4 or 5 slashes diagonally across each mackerel with a sharp knife, scoring through the skin into the flesh. Season with salt and pepper. Preheat the grill to high.

2 Melt the butter in a heavy-based pan. Add the gooseberries with the sugar, cover and cook over a medium heat for about 5–6 minutes, stirring every so often, until the gooseberries are soft and have broken down. Add the white wine, turn up the heat and cook until all the liquid has evaporated. Add the cream, bring to the boil and simmer until the sauce has reduced by half and thickened. Depending on the gooseberries, you may need to add a little more sugar.

3 Meanwhile, brush the mackerel with a little oil and cook under the hot grill for about 6–8 minutes. Transfer to warm plates and serve the gooseberry sauce separately, or on the plate if you like.

monkfish with cockles and mussels

Cockles in vinegar in little polystyrene pots bring back memories of being by the seaside. Fresh cockles, though, are sweet and delicious. If you can find live ones, they will need washing well to remove any sand. The best way to do this is to keep them under cold running water for an hour, giving them an occasional stir with your hand, allowing them to release as much sand as possible and allowing you to enjoy the experience. Otherwise, simply use clams or more mussels instead. Monkfish is becoming increasingly expensive owing to increasing demand, but any firm white fish will work equally well here.

Illustrated on previous page

SERVES 4

4 monkfish fillets, each about 200g (7oz)
1–2 tablespoons vegetable oil
150g (5oz) cockles or clams, rinsed
125g (4oz) mussels, scrubbed and any
  beards removed
1/2 glass of white wine
1 tablespoon chopped parsley
75g (3oz) unsalted butter, diced
sea salt and freshly ground black pepper

1 If the monkfish pieces are very thick, preheat the oven to 230°C (fan oven 210°C), gas mark 8 and a roasting pan. Whatever their thickness, lightly season the monkfish with salt and pepper. Heat a little oil in a large non-stick frying pan and fry the fillets for about 3 minutes on each side, until they are nicely coloured. Transfer very thick fillets to the hot roasting pan and finish cooking in the hot oven for another 5–10 minutes, or until cooked.

2 Meanwhile, give the cockles and mussels a final rinse, discarding any mussels that stay open when given a sharp tap. Put them into a large pan with the white wine and cover with a tight-fitting lid. Cook over a high heat for 3–4 minutes until they open, shaking the pan frequently and giving them an occasional stir. Drain in a colander, reserving the liquid, then pour it back into the pan.

3 Add the parsley and butter to the pan and keep stirring until the butter has melted. Return the molluscs to the pan, discarding any that haven't opened, adjust the seasoning and stir well.

4 To serve, carefully remove the monkfish from the pan with a fish slice and place on warm plates. Add the mussels and cockles, then spoon the parsley butter over the top to serve.

fillet of cod with parsley sauce

This classic dish needs only simple cooking and lots of parsley that's been freshly chopped – and, if possible, freshly picked. Supermarkets sell large pots of parsley and other herbs, so you can keep them on your windowsill or just outside the kitchen door. Cod loins, which are the thick cut at the top end of the fillet, are readily available these days and work perfectly for this dish, but you can use other firm-fleshed white fish, such as hake and pollack.

SERVES 4

4 boneless, skinless thick cod loin portions,
  each about 160–175g (5^1/$_2$–6oz)
good knob of softened butter
sea salt and freshly ground white pepper

FOR THE PARSLEY SAUCE:
good knob of butter
2 shallots, peeled and finely chopped
2 tablespoons white wine
150ml (^{1}/$_4$ pint) fish stock
400ml (14fl oz) double cream
2 tablespoons chopped parsley

1   Preheat the oven to 200°C (fan oven 180°C), gas mark 6. To make the sauce, melt the butter in a heavy-based pan and gently cook the shallots over a low heat for about 1 minute, until soft. Add the white wine and fish stock, and simmer until reduced to about a tablespoon or so. Add the cream and simmer until the sauce is reduced at least by half and is thick. Add the parsley and simmer for another minute or so to let it infuse. Season with salt and pepper to taste.

2   Meanwhile, season the cod fillets with salt and pepper, put them into an ovenproof dish and rub with softened butter. Bake for 10–15 minutes or until just cooked. Remove and drain on kitchen paper.

3   Place the cod portions on warm plates and spoon the parsley sauce over them. Serve accompanied by steamed spinach and/or mashed potato.

fish pie

A medley of fish in a piquant sauce is baked under a cheesy potato crust for a comforting pie that's best served simply with buttered spinach or peas. Make individual pies if you prefer.

SERVES 4–6

250g (9oz) cod or haddock fillet, skinned
250g (9oz) salmon fillet, skinned
250g (9oz) smoked cod or haddock fillet
500ml (16fl oz) fish stock
100ml (3 1/2 fl oz) white wine
2 tablespoons chopped parsley

FOR THE SAUCE:
50g (2oz) butter
50g (2oz) flour
175ml (6fl oz) double cream
2 teaspoons English mustard
1/2 tablespoon Worcestershire sauce
1 teaspoon anchovy essence
sea salt and freshly ground white pepper

FOR THE TOPPING:
1.5kg (3 1/4 lb) potatoes, peeled, cooked and
  mashed (see page 139)
50g (2oz) butter, softened
about 1–2 tablespoons milk
25g (1oz) fresh white breadcrumbs
25g (1oz) grated Cheddar cheese

1   Remove any small pin bones from the fish fillets, then cut roughly into 3cm (1 1/4 inch) chunks. Pour the fish stock and white wine into a large pan and bring to a simmer. Add the fish and poach gently in the liquid for 2 minutes. Drain in a colander over a bowl to save the liquor and leave to cool.

2   To make the sauce, melt the butter in a heavy-based pan over a low heat, then stir in the flour. Gradually stir in the reserved poaching liquor. Bring to the boil and simmer gently for 15 minutes.

3   Add the cream and continue to simmer for 10 minutes or so until the sauce has a thick coating consistency. Stir in the mustard, Worcestershire sauce, anchovy essence, and seasoning if required. Leave to cool for about 15 minutes.

4   Gently fold the cooked fish and parsley into the sauce, and spoon into a large pie dish to about 3cm (1 1/4 inches) from the rim. Leave to stand for about 30 minutes.

5   Preheat the oven to 180°C (fan oven 160°C), gas mark 4. To prepare the topping, mix the butter and milk into the mashed potato and season with a little salt and pepper. Spoon the potato over the pie and bake for 30 minutes, then scatter the breadcrumbs and cheese on top and bake for a further 15 minutes until golden.

fish cakes with tartare sauce

Fish cakes are an excellent way to use cheaper varieties of fish and off-cuts. You can make mini-versions of these to serve with drinks.

SERVES 4

325g (11oz) skinless fish fillets, such as salmon, smoked haddock and/or white fish

325g (11oz) simple mashed potato, without added milk or butter (page 139)

1/2 tablespoon anchovy essence

1/2 tablespoon English mustard

1 tablespoon chopped parsley

1 tablespoon chopped chives

flour, to dust

1 medium egg, beaten

50–65g (2–2¹/₂oz) fresh white breadcrumbs

vegetable oil, to fry

sea salt and freshly ground white pepper

FOR THE TARTARE SAUCE:

25g (1oz) gherkins, finely chopped

25g (1oz) capers, rinsed and finely chopped

1/2 tablespoon chopped parsley

4 tablespoons mayonnaise

squeeze of lemon juice

1 Poach the fish gently in salted water for 3–4 minutes, then drain and allow to cool. Flake the fish, checking for any small pin bones as you do so. In a bowl, mix half of the fish with the potato, anchovy essence, mustard, parsley, chives and salt and pepper until smooth. Gently fold in the remaining fish.

2 Mould the mixture into 4 large round cakes or 8 small ones and refrigerate for about 1 hour. Meanwhile mix together the ingredients for the tartare sauce in a bowl, cover and set aside.

3 Take 3 shallow bowls, put the flour in one, the egg in another and the breadcrumbs in the third. Lightly flour the fish cakes, dip them into the beaten egg, then into the breadcrumbs, shaking off excess each time. Shallow-fry the fish cakes in a 1cm (1/2 inch) depth of hot oil until crisp and golden, turning halfway through cooking, or deep-fry in oil at 175–180°C. Drain on kitchen paper and serve with the tartare sauce.

baked herrings with mustard and oats

Herrings were plentiful and cheap around our coastlines in times past, especially along the East Anglian coast. In the twelfth century, Great Yarmouth became the centre of the herring trade and the fish were cured in barrels of salt, pickled, and smoked as bloaters. Nowadays, herring fishing is restricted in the North Sea because of overfishing, so these fish are a less common sight on fishmongers' slabs.

SERVES 4

40g (1¹/₂oz) butter
2 shallots, peeled and finely chopped
finely grated zest of ¹/₂ unwaxed lemon
40g (1¹/₂oz) fresh white breadcrumbs
40g (1¹/₂oz) oat flakes
1 tablespoon chopped parsley
4 herring fillets, each about 150g (5oz), or
   8 smaller ones
1 tablespoon grainy mustard
sea salt and freshly ground black pepper

1   Preheat the oven to 200°C (fan oven 180°C), gas mark 6. Melt the butter in a pan and gently cook the shallots for a couple of minutes until soft. Transfer to a food processor with the lemon zest, breadcrumbs, oats and parsley. Season with salt and pepper and process for about 20 seconds.

2   Check over the herring fillets and remove any small bones, then place on a baking tray, skin-side up. Spread the mustard evenly over the fillets and spoon the oat mixture on top, pressing it down with the back of the spoon. Bake for 15–20 minutes until cooked. Serve with hot buttered new potatoes.

kedgeree

The Hindi dish of *khichri* has come a long way and developed itself – or, rather, the British in India developed it – into the breakfast dish that it is today. Smoked Finnan haddock makes the best kedgeree by far, as the smokiness travels through the sauce and rice to give that delicious savoury flavour. Don't be tempted to buy dyed yellow haddock fillet, as no smoke on this earth can ever produce that colour. If you fancy it, though, do replace a little smoked haddock with salmon fillet as this gives a good contrast in colour and flavour. Even a few prawns thrown in adds a luxurious little extra.

SERVES 4

350g (12oz) undyed smoked haddock fillet

150g (5oz) basmati rice

1 tablespoon chopped parsley

3 medium eggs, hard-boiled, shelled and
   chopped

FOR THE CURRY SAUCE:

25g (1oz) butter

2 shallots, peeled and finely chopped

small piece of fresh root ginger, peeled and
   finely chopped

1 garlic clove, peeled and crushed

¼ teaspoon ground turmeric

¼ teaspoon ground cumin

½ teaspoon curry powder

½ teaspoon fennel seeds

few curry leaves

pinch of saffron threads

100ml (3½fl oz) fish stock

400ml (14fl oz) double cream

sea salt and freshly ground black pepper

1 First make the curry sauce. Melt the butter in a heavy-based pan, add the shallots, ginger and garlic and cook gently until softened, without allowing them to colour. Add the ground spices, fennel seeds, curry leaves and saffron threads, and cook for another minute to release their flavours. Add the fish stock, bring to the boil and allow it to reduce by half. Pour in the cream and simmer until reduced by half. Blend the sauce in a blender or using a hand-held blender until smooth, then pass it through a fine-meshed sieve. Adjust the seasoning, if necessary.

2 Poach the smoked haddock in a pan of gently simmering, lightly salted water for 3–4 minutes, then remove from the heat. Leave the fish to cool in the liquid.

3 Rinse the rice a couple times in cold water to remove excess starch, then cook in plenty of boiling salted water for 12–15 minutes until just tender. Briefly drain the rice in a colander, return it to the pan, put the lid on and leave off the heat for few minutes. This allows the rice to steam dry and gives it a light fluffy texture.

4 To serve the kedgeree, reheat the curry sauce. Drain the smoked haddock and flake the flesh, then add to the sauce with the chopped parsley. Put the rice into a bowl, spoon over the fish and sauce, then scatter over the chopped hard-boiled egg.

4 poultry and game

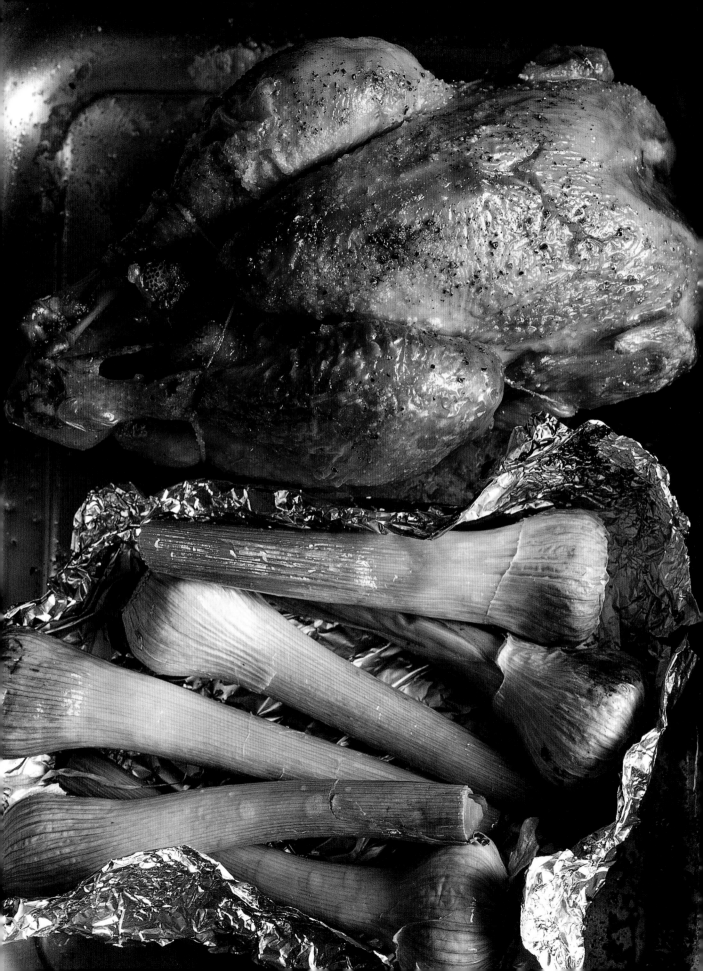

roast chicken with baked garlic and parsley sauce

I discovered this sauce by mistake when I was roasting some rather large healthy-looking chickens with whole new season's fresh garlic bulbs – one of the joys of spring. It seemed a shame to waste the tasty fat in the roasting tin. I knew of an Italian recipe with bone marrow, garlic and grated Parmesan, called *la perla*, which is traditionally served with boiled meats or *bolito misto*. This prompted me to experiment and blend some of the cooked tender garlic bulbs with the excess chicken fat, some breadcrumbs and parsley, and a little Parmesan cheese to give it a nice savoury flavour. I know the idea is not strictly British, but the ingredients certainly are (except if you use Parmesan, of course).

SERVES 4

1 chicken, preferably free-range, organic or
   corn-fed, about 1.5kg (3¼lb)
few thyme sprigs
olive oil, to brush
sea salt and freshly ground black pepper

FOR THE BAKED GARLIC AND PARSLEY SAUCE:

4–6 heads of new season's garlic
chicken fat and juices from the roasting pan or
   100g (3½oz) canned duck or goose fat
handful of flat leaf parsley
about 1 tablespoon English mustard
65g (2½oz) fresh white breadcrumbs
25g (1oz) Cheddar or Parmesan cheese, grated

1 Preheat the oven to 200°C (fan oven 180°C), gas mark 6. Season the chicken inside and out, pop the thyme in its cavity and brush the bird lightly all over with olive oil. Place in a lightly oiled roasting tin, resting the bird on one leg, rather than upright.

2 Roast the chicken in the oven. After 25 minutes turn the chicken on to the other leg and roast for another 25 minutes, then finish cooking breast uppermost. Wrap the garlic for the sauce in a foil parcel and bake with the chicken for about 1 hour. Test the chicken after 1¼ hours: the juices should run clear when a skewer or knife tip is inserted into the thickest part of the thigh.

3 When cooked, transfer the chicken to a warm platter. Leave to rest in a warm place for 15 minutes.

4 To make the sauce, remove the outer skin from the garlic. Warm the fat and juices in the roasting tin, then put into a blender or food processor with the garlic, parsley, mustard and breadcrumbs. Whiz until smooth and season with salt and pepper. Add a little more cheese and mustard to taste if you wish. Pour any juices from the rested chicken into the sauce and thin with a little water if the sauce is too thick.

5 Carve the chicken and serve with the garlic and parsley sauce, and vegetables of your choice.

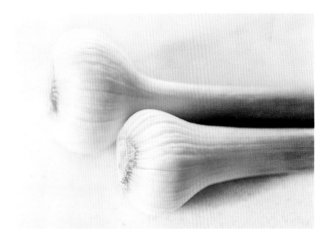

guinea fowl with Savoy cabbage and mushrooms

Once a rarity, now the bohemian of the poultry yard, the guinea fowl has a delicious flavour somewhere between pheasant and the best flavoured chicken you can buy. Unfortunately, it still doesn't grace many home tables, due to the competition of chicken and turkey. This is a real pity, as its moist, creamy yellow flesh is delicious and will withstand most robust garnishes.

SERVES 4

6 garlic cloves, peeled

few thyme sprigs

2 guinea fowl, each about 1.1kg (2½lb)

125g (4oz) butter

4 tablespoons red wine

4 tablespoons port

150ml (¼ pint) chicken stock

1–2 teaspoons cornflour (optional)

1kg (2¼lb) Savoy cabbage, trimmed, cored
  and roughly chopped

200g (7oz) wild mushrooms, cleaned, trimmed
  and halved or quartered

1 tablespoon chopped parsley

sea salt and freshly ground black pepper

1   Preheat the oven to 220°C (fan oven 200°C), gas mark 7. Divide the garlic cloves and thyme between the cavities of the two birds. Rub the breasts with 25g (1oz) of the butter and season well with salt and pepper. Place in a roasting tin and roast for 1 hour, basting occasionally.

2   Transfer the guinea fowl to a plate, cover with foil and set aside to rest. Put the roasting tin on a medium heat on the hob, add the red wine and port, and stir well to scrape up any residue on the bottom of the tin. Add the stock and simmer for 3–4 minutes, then strain through a fine sieve. (If you want a thicker gravy, mix the cornflour with a little cold water, add to the gravy and simmer, stirring, for another minute or so, before straining.)

3   While the birds are resting, cook the cabbage in boiling salted water for about 5 minutes, until tender. Drain and add 50g (2oz) of the butter, season with salt and pepper and cover with a lid.

4   In the meantime, heat the rest of the butter in a frying pan, add the mushrooms and parsley, season with salt and pepper and sauté over a medium heat until tender. Timing will depend on the type of wild mushrooms; chanterelles take only 30–40 seconds, whereas girolles will take a couple of minutes, for example.

5   To serve, remove the legs from the guinea fowl and cut the breasts away from the bone with a sharp knife. Arrange the cabbage on the plates, put the leg and breast meat on top, then pour the sauce around. Spoon the wild mushrooms on top and serve.

roasting poultry and game

Nowadays we seem to be rearing better free-range and corn-fed poultry, which cost more than their battery-reared cousins, but taste far superior. Of course, final flavour is down to the cooking, and a well seasoned bird is a good starting point.

Game birds are one of those autumnal treats. Be it partridge, grouse or pheasant, only young game birds should be selected for roasting and these are best cooked simply, and served pink. Quick roasting at a high temperature will keep smaller birds moist and tender, overcooking will make them dry. If you prefer game well cooked, protect the breasts with streaky bacon rashers, especially pheasant.

For me, spit-roasting is the best way of roasting, as you get a good even heat and the cooking time is shorter. If your oven doesn't have a spit-roaster, you can suspend the bird on a rack that fits in the roasting tin to allow it to cook evenly and crisp up.

Guide to roasting

Chicken
For a 1.2–1.5kg (2¾–3¼lb) bird, allow 40 minutes per kilo (20 minutes per pound), plus an extra 15 minutes, about 1¼ hours in total, at 200°C (fan oven 180°C), gas mark 6. Rest for 15 minutes.

Turkey
For a 4.5–5.5kg (10–12lb) bird, allow 30 minutes per kilo (15 minutes per pound) at 190°C (fan oven 170°C), gas mark 5. Rest for 30 minutes.

Pheasant
Rub the breasts with butter and cover with streaky bacon or pork fat. Cook for 25 minutes at 200°C (fan oven 180°C), gas mark 6. Rest for 5 minutes.

Grouse, snipe, partridge, wood pigeon
Rub the breasts with butter and roast at a high heat, 220°C (fan oven 200°C), gas mark 7, for 15–20 minutes for pink game, or a little longer for well cooked game. Roast mallard in the same way, but allow 30 minutes. Rest for 5 minutes.

stuffings for poultry

Homemade stuffings are easy and taste delicious. Just keep some fresh breadcrumbs in the freezer for your base. I like to add some sautéed chopped chicken livers to my stuffing, but you can vary the mix as you wish – adding a little grated lemon zest perhaps, or replace the thyme with some chopped sage leaves for a more traditional sage and onion stuffing, or add chestnuts for turkey. Stuff the neck end of the bird only.

bread sauce

To serve 4, cook a diced ½ onion in 25g (1oz) butter until soft. Add the other ½ onion studded with 3 cloves, each pushed through a bay leaf. Add 500ml (16fl oz) milk, pinch of nutmeg and seasoning. Simmer for 15 minutes. Infuse off the heat for 30 minutes. Discard studded onion. Add 100g (3½oz) fresh white breadcrumbs and simmer for 10 minutes. Whiz a third in a blender, return to pan and stir in 25g (1oz) butter; season.

▲ parsley, thyme and onion stuffing

To make enough to stuff a large chicken to serve 4, gently cook a finely chopped onion and 2 tsp chopped thyme in 50g (2oz) butter for a few minutes until soft, without allowing it to colour. Off the heat, stir in 125g (4oz) fresh white breadcrumbs and 2 tbsp chopped parsley. Season with salt and black pepper. Stuff the neck end of the bird only.

▲ pan gravy

Tip out as much of the fat from the roasting pan as you can, then place on a medium heat. Add a splash of dry red or white wine, perhaps dust with a little flour, then stir in a cupful of stock. Scrape up the sediment from the bottom and cook rapidly for a minute or so. For a thicker gravy, add a spoonful of cornflour mixed with a little cold water and simmer for 1 minute. Adjust the seasoning and stir in a knob of butter to give the gravy a sheen.

roast Gressingham duck with apple sauce

Apple sauce is a perfect marriage to roast duck as it cuts the fat with its sweet and slightly acidic flavour. Roasting a quality duck is fairly effortless as it takes little cooking and there is not too much fat to contend with. Serve this with some roast potatoes – cooked in the pan with the duck.

SERVES 4

2 ducks, preferably Gressingham, each about
    1.5–2kg (3$^1/_4$–4$^1/_2$lb)
4 garlic cloves
few thyme sprigs
few rosemary sprigs
sea salt and freshly ground black pepper

TO SERVE:

Bramley apple sauce (page 114)
basic gravy (see below)

1 Preheat the oven to 220°C (fan oven 200°C), gas mark 7. Place the ducks on a board. Divide the garlic, thyme and rosemary between their cavities and season them inside and out with salt and pepper. Place side by side in a roasting tin and roast for 1 hour.

2 Meanwhile, make the apple sauce. If you get giblets with the duck, then simmer them in the gravy for about 10 minutes.

3 To serve, remove the legs from the duck, then take the breasts off the bone and cut into 3 or 4 slices, or simply cut the birds in half and serve them on the bone. Serve with the apple sauce and gravy.

basic gravy It's a good idea to make a sizeable quantity of gravy every so often. Freeze it in small plastic pots and you can defrost it for instant proper gravy to go with a roast. Keep some frozen in ice-cube trays to use in smaller quantities for enhancing sauces.

To make about 2 litres (3½ pints), you will need 2kg (4½lb) beef, veal, lamb or chicken bones, or a mixture, depending on intended use, chopped into small pieces. Preheat the oven to 200°C (fan oven 180°C), gas mark 6. Roughly chop 3 peeled onions, 5 peeled carrots, a few celery stalks, 2 leeks (rinse well) and ½ head of garlic, then place in a roasting tin with the bones. Roast for about 15–20 minutes until golden brown, giving them a good stir every so often. Add 1 tablespoon tomato purée, then sprinkle in 2 tablespoons flour and stir well. Roast for another 10 minutes.

Meanwhile, measure 3–4 litres (5–7 pints) dark meat stock (page 21) or make up this quantity of stock using good quality cubes. Put the roasting tin on the hob, add a little of the stock and stir over a low heat, scraping up the sediment from the bottom. Transfer everything to a large saucepan and pour in the rest of the stock to cover. Add 10 black peppercorns, a few thyme sprigs and a bay leaf. Bring to the boil and skim off any scum from the surface. Simmer for 2 hours, topping up with water to keep the ingredients covered and skimming occasionally as required.

Strain through a fine-meshed sieve and remove any fat from the surface. Taste to check the strength and boil to reduce and concentrate the flavour if necessary. If the gravy is not thick enough, dilute 1-2 teaspoons cornflour in a little cold water, stir in and simmer, stirring, for a few minutes.

chicken, ham and leek pie

In winter, a home-cooked pie with some mashed root vegetables or mashed potato is certainly worth rushing home for. It can be made a couple of days in advance and stored in the fridge.

SERVES 4

600ml (1 pint) chicken stock
500g (1lb 2oz) skinless chicken thigh fillets
3 large leeks, trimmed, roughly chopped and
   rinsed
40g (1½oz) butter
40g (1½oz) plain flour

100ml (3½fl oz) double cream
200g (7oz) good quality ham, trimmed of fat
   (preferably home-cooked, see page 112)
2 tablespoons chopped parsley
350–400g (12–14oz) good quality puff pastry
1 medium egg, beaten
sea salt and freshly ground white pepper

1   Pour the chicken stock into a shallow pan and bring to the boil. Lower the heat, add the chicken thighs and poach gently for 10 minutes. Remove with a slotted spoon and put to one side.

2   Add the leeks to the chicken stock and simmer gently for 10 minutes, then drain in a colander over a bowl to retain the stock.

3   Melt the butter in a heavy-based pan, add the flour and stir well. Gradually add the reserved stock, stirring constantly to avoid lumps. Bring to the boil, season with a little salt and pepper, and simmer gently for about 5 minutes, stirring every so often. Add the cream, bring back to the boil and simmer for a further 5 minutes. The sauce should be quite thick by now; if not, simmer a little longer until it is, then leave to cool.

4   Cut the ham roughly into 2cm (¾ inch) cubes. Add to the cooled sauce with the leeks, chicken and parsley. Adjust the seasoning, then spoon into 4 individual pie dishes, or one large one to 1cm (½ inch) from the top.

5   Roll the puff pastry out on a floured surface to a 5mm (¼ inch) thickness. Cut out top(s) for the pie(s) about 2cm (¾ inch) larger all the way round than the dish(es). Brush the edges of the pastry with a little of the beaten egg. Lay the pastry over the top of the pie dish(es), pressing the egg-washed sides against the rim. Cut a small slit in the top of each pie to allow steam to escape and brush with beaten egg. Leave to rest in a cool place for 30 minutes.

6   Preheat the oven to 200°C (fan oven 180°C), gas mark 6. Cook the pie(s) for 40–50 minutes until the pastry is golden. Serve hot.

braised duck with peas

Try to buy good quality ducks like Gressingham or Barbary, as they are reared with less fat and a higher meat content. When fresh peas are in season, make sure you use them – you'll need to buy about 600g (1¼lb) peas in the pod.

SERVES 4

2 good quality ducks, such as Gressingham, each
   about 1.5–2kg (3¼–4½lb)
200ml (7fl oz) sweet cider
600ml (1 pint) basic gravy (page 88)
600ml (1 pint) chicken stock

few thyme sprigs
1 bay leaf
2 tablespoons double cream
200g (7oz) shelled fresh or frozen peas,
   freshly cooked
sea salt and freshly ground black pepper

1 Preheat the oven to 220°C (fan oven 200°C), gas mark 7. With a heavy chopping knife, cut the ducks in half. Cut the parson's nose off and trim away any excess fat and the backbone where there isn't any meat. Chop the knuckle from the legs and trim the wing bones, if necessary. Season the birds with salt and pepper, then roast them, skin-side down, in a roasting tin for 30 minutes. Transfer the ducks to a colander over a bowl to drain off the fat.

2 Turn the oven down to 170°C (fan oven 150°C), gas mark 3. Carefully cut the duck halves in half, where the breast joins the leg.

3 Put the duck pieces into a casserole dish with the cider, gravy, chicken stock, thyme and bay leaf. Cover with a lid and braise for 1¼ hours. Remove the ducks from the liquid with a slotted spoon, put them on a warm plate and cover with foil. Set aside.

4 Transfer the cooking liquid to a saucepan, skim off any fat and simmer until reduced and thickened. Return the duck to the liquid, add the cream and peas just to warm through, then check the seasoning and serve.

cock-a-leekie

This ancient dish is usually attributed to the Scots but is also sometimes claimed by the Welsh. Traditionally, this sort of soupy stew would be made with some shin of beef and a boiling fowl or capon for the base stock, then the meat would be used in other dishes as well as serving in the soup itself. If you want to use a boiling fowl or capon then fine, although the breast meat as a meal can be a bit dry. Chicken legs work well in this recipe as they have the most flavour and make a good broth.

Illustrated on previous page

SERVES 4

*200g (7oz) piece of stewing beef, such as shin
or flank*
2 litres (3½ pints) chicken stock
*200g (7oz) large leeks, halved lengthways
and rinsed*
4 chicken legs, skinned
*16 large good quality pitted prunes, soaked in
warm water overnight*
*150g (5oz) small finger leeks, halved if long
and rinsed*
sea salt and freshly ground black pepper

1 Put the beef into a saucepan with the chicken stock. Add the large leeks, trimming them to fit the pan if necessary. Bring to the boil and skim off any scum that forms on the surface. Season with salt and pepper, then simmer gently for 1½ hours.

2 Meanwhile, cut the chicken legs in half at the joint, and chop the knuckles off the drumsticks. Add the chicken legs to the pan and simmer for another 30 minutes.

3 Drain though a colander into a bowl and reserve the chicken and beef, discarding the leeks. Skim the stock and strain through a fine sieve into a clean pan. Add the prunes and finger leeks. Cut the beef into 4 pieces and return to the pan with the chicken. Simmer for another 15 minutes, until the leeks are tender. Adjust the seasoning, if necessary.

4 Serve the cock-a-leekie as it is or, for a more refined soup, remove the chicken from the bone, shred the meat and return to the soup.

Kentish pudding

Originally this dish would have been made using a boiling fowl, but boneless chicken thighs are perfect for the long slow cooking method as they keep their shape and don't dry out. You can vary the mushrooms as you please – girolles, for example, would give a great colour and flavour to the finished sauce.

SERVES 4–6

FOR THE SUET PASTRY:
275g (10oz) self-raising flour, plus extra to dust
140g (4¹/₂oz) suet
¹/₂ teaspoon salt

FOR THE FILLING:
750g (1lb 10oz) boneless skinless chicken
  thighs, halved
50g (2oz) butter, plus extra to grease
1 large onion, peeled and finely chopped

100g (3¹/₂oz) rindless smoked streaky bacon, cut
  into 2cm (³/₄ inch) pieces
250g (9oz) button mushrooms, halved or
  quartered, depending on size
3 tablespoons flour, plus extra to dust
4 tablespoons white wine
350ml (12fl oz) chicken stock
2 tablespoons chopped parsley
sea salt and freshly ground black pepper

1   To make the suet pastry, mix the flour, suet and salt together in a bowl, then mix to a soft dough with about 100ml (3¹/₂fl oz) cold water. Roll out to a circle large enough to line a 2 litre (3¹/₂ pint) pudding basin. Cut a quarter out of the circle for the lid and to ease the lining of the bowl. Grease the pudding basin well with butter, drop the larger piece of pastry into it and join up the edges where the quarter was removed. Trim the edges around the bowl.

2   Season the chicken with salt and pepper and flour lightly. Melt 15g (¹/₂oz) of the butter in a large frying pan and cook the chicken pieces for a couple of minutes on each side without allowing them to colour (you may need to do this in 2 batches). Remove from the pan and put to one side.

3   Melt the rest of the butter in the pan, add the onion and bacon, and cook gently until soft, then add the mushrooms and cook for another 2–3 minutes, stirring well, until they soften. Add the flour, stir well, then slowly stir in the wine and stock and bring to the boil, stirring. Remove from the heat and leave to cool.

4   Add the chicken and parsley to the sauce, mix well and adjust the seasoning. Tip the mixture into the lined pudding basin. Remould the pastry for the lid and roll it out to the correct size. Lay it over the filling and press the edges together to seal in the filling, trimming as necessary.

5   Cover the top generously with a piece of pleated foil and secure under the rim with string, making a handle so the pudding basin can be lifted easily. Lower the pudding into a pan containing enough boiling water to come about halfway up the side of the basin. Cover with a lid and simmer very gently for 4 hours, topping up with more boiling water as necessary. Lift out the pudding, remove the foil and serve straight from the basin.

pot-roast pheasant with chestnuts

Removing the breasts from the pheasant gives a much more succulent result, as the cooking can then be better controlled. Stuffing the breasts can also help disguise any slight dryness of the flesh. Try to buy smaller, younger birds earlier in the season, as these will be more tender.

SERVES 4

4 plump boneless pheasant breasts, with skin
100g (3½oz) freshly shelled or vacuum-packed
   chestnuts, roughly chopped
2 shallots, peeled and finely chopped
40g (1½oz) fresh white breadcrumbs
1 tablespoon chopped parsley
25g (1oz) butter, melted

1 tablespoon vegetable oil
sea salt and freshly ground black pepper

TO SERVE:
creamed Brussels sprouts (page 130)
150ml (¼ pint) pan gravy (page 87, made with
   red wine)
parsnip chips (see below)

1 Preheat the oven to 200°C (fan oven 180°C), gas mark 6. Lay the pheasant breasts on a board, skin-side down. Remove the fillet and put to one side. With the tip of a sharp knife, cut two incisions away from the centre of the breast to form a pocket. (Basically you are just transferring some of the breast meat away from the middle of the breast to make room for the stuffing.)

2 Mix the chestnuts, shallots, breadcrumbs, parsley and melted butter together and season with salt and pepper. Divide the stuffing between the 4 breasts. Flatten the fillet a little with the side of your hand and lay it over the stuffing. Fold the breast meat that you cut previously back into the centre to completely seal in the stuffing.

3 Heat the oil in a roasting tin in the oven for a few minutes. Season the pheasant breasts, then place in the hot tin and cook in the oven for 5–7 minutes on each side, or until cooked to your liking.

4 Remove the pheasant from the oven and carve into slices. Serve on a bed of creamed Brussels sprouts, with the red wine pan gravy and a few parsnip chips.

parsnip chips Using a mandolin grater or swivel vegetable peeler, slice 2 trimmed parsnips as thinly as possible lengthways, rinse well and pat dry with a clean tea towel. Half-fill a deep-fat fryer or deep, heavy-based saucepan with oil and heat to 180°C. Deep-fry the parsnip slices, a handful at a time, for 2–3 minutes until golden, stirring to ensure they don't stick together. Remove and place on kitchen paper to dry out and crisp up. Sprinkle with salt and leave in a warm (not hot) place while you cook the rest.

game pie

Game for pies is traditionally a mixture of game birds, rabbit, hare and diced venison. As these take different times to cook, I find the best solution is to use a mixture of game bird thighs and tender cuts from the leg of venison. You'll need to marinate the meat a couple of days in advance.

SERVES 4

1kg (2¼lb) boneless game meat

2 glasses of good red wine

1 garlic clove, peeled and crushed

1 teaspoon chopped thyme

4 juniper berries, crushed

1 bay leaf

2 tablespoons vegetable oil

2 tablespoons plain flour

25g (1oz) butter

1 large onion, peeled and finely chopped

1 teaspoon tomato purée

1 litre (1¾ pints) beef stock

350–400g (12–14oz) good quality puff pastry

1 medium egg, beaten

sea salt and freshly ground black pepper

1   About 2 days ahead, cut the game roughly into 3cm (1¼ inch) cubes and put into a stainless steel (or other non-reactive) bowl with the red wine, garlic, thyme, juniper berries and bay leaf. Cover with cling film and marinate in the fridge for 2 days.

2   Drain the meat in a colander over a bowl, reserving the marinade, and dry the pieces on kitchen paper. Heat the oil in a large heavy-based frying pan until almost smoking. Meanwhile, lightly flour the meat with ½ tablespoon of the flour, seasoned with salt and pepper. Fry the meat in 2 or 3 batches over a high heat until nicely browned, then remove and set aside.

3   Heat the butter in the pan and gently fry the onion until soft. Add the remaining flour and tomato purée and stir over a low heat for a minute. Slowly stir in the marinade and stock. Bring to the boil, add the meat, cover and simmer gently for 1–2 hours, or until the meat is tender. Or cook in the oven at 170°C (fan oven 150°C), gas mark 3. Start checking the meat after 1 hour; it's difficult to put an exact time on braised meats. Once it is cooked, the sauce should have thickened to the consistency of gravy. (If not, thicken with 1–2 teaspoons cornflour mixed with a little cold water and simmer briefly, stirring.)

4   Allow the game mixture to cool, then use to fill a large pie dish, to 1 cm (½ inch) from the rim, discarding the bay leaf.

5   Roll out the pastry on a floured surface to a 5mm (¼ inch) thickness and cut out a round or oval, about 2cm (¾ inch) larger all round than the pie dish. Brush the pastry edges with a little beaten egg. Lay the pastry on top of the dish, pushing the sides against the rim. Cut a small slit in the top to allow steam to escape and brush with beaten egg. Leave to rest in a cool place for 30 minutes. Meanwhile, preheat the oven to 200°C (fan oven 180°C), gas mark 6. Cook the pie for 40–50 minutes, until the pastry is crisp and golden.

wild rabbit cooked in cider

Wild rabbits are generally sold whole. It seems a shame, though, to cook them whole as the saddles take much less time than the legs to cook and therefore tend to be a bit dry. Remove the front and back legs, or get your butcher to do it, and keep the saddles for a salad. Once removed from the bone, the saddle fillets take only a few minutes to cook. They are really tender and make a great starter with some pan-fried black pudding, seasonal leaves and a good mustard dressing. If wild rabbits are not available, buy tender farmed rabbits instead. These are about twice the size of the wild, so one leg is almost enough for one person.

SERVES 4

12 rabbit legs (back legs only)
40g (1¹/₂oz) flour, plus extra to dust
2 tablespoons vegetable oil
25g (1oz) butter
1 onion, peeled and roughly chopped
400ml (14fl oz) dry cider
750ml (1¹/₄ pints) chicken stock
3 tablespoons double cream
1 tablespoon chopped parsley
sea salt and freshly ground black pepper

1   Halve the rabbit legs at the joint, then lightly flour them and season with salt and pepper. Heat the oil in a frying pan, add the rabbit legs and brown lightly on both sides, then drain on kitchen paper.

2   Heat the butter in a heavy-based saucepan, add the onion and cook gently until soft. Add the flour and stir well. Gradually add the cider, stirring well, then add the chicken stock. Bring to the boil, add the rabbit legs and season lightly with salt and pepper. Cover the pan and simmer gently for 1¹/₄ hours or until the rabbit is tender.

3   Remove the rabbit legs with a slotted spoon and set aside. Add the cream to the cooking liquor and continue to simmer until the sauce has thickened. Put the legs back into the sauce with the parsley and bring back to the boil. Serve with some good mashed potato or a mashed root vegetable.

roast saddle of venison with haggis and bashed neeps

The saddle is the most tender readily available cut of venison and, of course, the most expensive. It doesn't take much cooking once removed from the bone, and it eats like the best fillet steak with a little hint of game. You can roast it on the bone, but as the eye of meat is generally so small, a few minutes in a pan is all it really needs. The gaminess of venison depends on how young it is or how long it's been hung, and it is very much a matter of personal preference. Either way I like to marinate it overnight in red wine, with a few crushed juniper berries and some thyme leaves.

SERVES 4

4 trimmed venison saddle fillets, each about
    150g (5oz)
1/2 glass of good red wine
6 juniper berries, crushed
few thyme sprigs, chopped
1–2 tablespoons vegetable oil
150ml (1/4 pint) pan gravy (page 87) or
    basic gravy (page 88)

FOR THE BASHED NEEPS:

250g (9oz) parsnips, peeled and roughly
    chopped
250g (9oz) swede, peeled and roughly chopped
150–200g (5–7oz) good quality haggis, skin
    removed
good knob of butter
sea salt and freshly ground black pepper

1 A day in advance, put the venison in a stainless steel (or other non-reactive) bowl with the wine, juniper and thyme, cover with cling film and leave to marinate overnight.

2 Next day, prepare the neeps: put the parsnips and swede into a pan, add water to cover and season with salt and pepper. Bring to the boil and simmer gently for 15–20 minutes, until soft enough to mash. Meanwhile cut the haggis roughly into 1cm (1/2 inch) pieces and set aside. Drain the vegetables in a colander, then tip into a bowl and coarsely mash with a potato masher. Add the butter and haggis, adjust the seasoning if necessary, and stir well.

3 Remove the venison from the marinade, reserving the liquid. Pat the fillets dry on some kitchen paper and season with salt and pepper. Heat a little vegetable oil in a heavy-based frying pan and cook the fillets for 2–3 minutes on each side for medium rare; allow an extra 1–2 minutes each side for medium or longer if the fillets are very thick. Leave to rest on a warm plate.

4 Meanwhile, boil the marinade in a saucepan rapidly until reduced to about a tablespoon. Add the gravy and any juices from the venison, and simmer for a minute or so until the sauce is thick, then strain through a fine sieve.

5 Reheat the bashed neeps and spoon into the centre of each warm serving plate. Slice the venison into 4 or 5 pieces and arrange on the neeps, then pour the sauce around.

5 meat

roast beef and Yorkshire pudding

A rib of beef, on or off the bone, is by far the best roasting joint as far as I'm concerned. It has some fat, but this really enhances the flavour. If cooking on the bone, you need a very large joint for 4–6 people, and space in the oven for Yorkshire pudding and potatoes, which may not be convenient at home. Instead I would recommend rib-eye, which is readily available these days.

Here the Yorkshire pudding is cooked whole, the old-fashioned way, so it's still a bit gooey in the middle. If you prefer crisp little puddings, cook the batter in individual Yorkshire pudding moulds at 230°C (fan oven 210°C), gas mark 8 while the beef is resting.

SERVES 4–6

1 rib-eye of beef off the bone, about 1–1.5kg
(2¼–3¼lb)
beef dripping, or vegetable oil, to roast
2 onions, peeled and halved
2 carrots, scrubbed or peeled and halved
sea salt and freshly ground black pepper

FOR THE YORKSHIRE PUDDING:
250g (9oz) plain flour
4 medium eggs, beaten
500–600ml (16fl oz–1 pint) milk

FOR THE GRAVY:
glass of red or white wine
200ml (7fl oz) beef stock

1 Preheat the oven to 220°C (fan oven 200°C), gas mark 7. Put a little dripping or oil into a large roasting tin and heat in the oven for 10 minutes. Season the beef and roast for 15 minutes, then turn it over to seal the meat and keep the juices in. Put the onions and carrots under the beef to act as a trivet (or use a steel trivet); this helps the beef to cook evenly and flavours the gravy. Allow 30 minutes per kg (13 minutes per lb) for rare; add another 10 minutes per kg (4 minutes per lb) for medium; or an extra 20 minutes per kg (6 minutes per lb) for well done. Baste the meat regularly with the pan juices.

2 Meanwhile, make the Yorkshire batter. Put the flour into a bowl and add a good pinch of salt. Mix in the eggs and a little of the milk with a whisk to form a paste. Mix in the rest of the milk, trying not to beat the batter too much, to give a thick pouring consistency.

3 About 25 minutes before the beef will be ready, pour some of the hot fat from the beef into a large roasting tin and heat in the oven for 5 minutes until smoking. Pour the batter into the roasting tin and bake for 30 minutes, until well risen and crisp on the outside.

4 Rest the beef for about 15 minutes before carving. To make the gravy, deglaze the roasting pan with the wine and add the stock. (If required thicken with 1–2 teaspoons cornflour mixed with a little water). Simmer, stirring, for 1–2 minutes. Serve the beef cut into thick slices, with the Yorkshire pudding and gravy.

steak and oyster pie

In this good old-fashioned dish, oysters replace kidneys to give the gravy a slight taste of the sea. You need to marinate the meat two days ahead. Serve with mash – plain or flavoured.

SERVES 4–6

800g (1¾lb) braising beef (flank, skirt or shin)
glass of good red wine
150ml (¼ pint) stout
1 garlic clove, peeled and crushed
1 teaspoon chopped thyme leaves
1 bay leaf
2 tablespoons vegetable oil
2 tablespoons plain flour

25g (1oz) butter
1 small onion, peeled and finely chopped
1 teaspoon tomato purée
1.5 litres (2½ pints) beef stock
4 or 8 rock oysters, opened and removed from
    their shells (see page 36)
350–400g (12–14oz) good quality puff pastry
1 medium egg, beaten
salt and freshly ground black pepper

1 Cut the beef into 3cm (1¼ inch) cubes and place in a non-reactive bowl with the wine, stout, garlic, thyme and bay leaf. Cover and marinate in the fridge for 2 days.

2 Drain meat, reserving marinade; pat dry. Heat the oil in a heavy frying pan. Season ½ tablespoon flour, lightly coat the meat and fry in batches over a high heat until browned. Heat the butter in a large heavy-based pan and gently fry the onion until soft. Add remaining flour and tomato purée; stir for 1 minute. Slowly stir in the marinade, then bring to a boil and reduce by half. Add the stock and beef, cover and simmer gently for 2–2½ hours, until the meat is tender and the sauce is a gravy-like consistency. If necessary, thicken with 1–2 teaspoons cornflour mixed with a little water and simmer, stirring, for 1–2 minutes. Cool, then use to fill 4 individual pie dishes to 1cm (½ inch) from the top. Add the oysters.

3 Roll out the pastry to a 5mm (¼ inch) thickness and cut out pie lids, 2cm (¾ inch) larger all round than the dishes. Brush the edges with egg and lay the pastry over the filling, pressing the edges on to the rims. Cut a slit in the middle and brush with egg. Rest in a cool place for 30 minutes. Preheat the oven to 200°C (fan oven 180°C), gas mark 6. Bake the pies for 40–50 minutes, until golden.

braised beef in Guinness

Start this dish a couple of days before you intend to serve it. Try to buy a whole piece of braising beef and cut it into 3–4cm (1¼–1½ inch) thick steaks. To soak up the delicious juices, serve with a potato dish like colcannon (page 138), or bashed neeps (page 101).

SERVES 4

4 thick-cut pieces of braising beef, preferably
    flank, skirt or shin, each about 250–300g
    (9–11oz)
glass of good red wine
150ml (¼ pint) Guinness
1 garlic clove, peeled and crushed
1 teaspoon chopped thyme leaves
1 bay leaf

2 tablespoons vegetable oil
1½ tablespoons plain flour
25g (1oz) butter
1 small onion, peeled and finely chopped
1 teaspoon tomato purée
1.2 litres (2 pints) beef stock
1 teaspoon cornflour (optional)
salt and freshly ground black pepper

1 Two days ahead, put the pieces of beef into a stainless steel (or other non-reactive) bowl with the red wine, Guinness, garlic, thyme and bay leaf. Cover with cling film and marinate in the fridge for 2 days.

2 Drain the meat in a colander over a bowl, reserving the marinade, and dry the pieces on kitchen paper. Heat the oil in a heavy frying pan. Meanwhile, lightly flour the meat with ½ tablespoon of the flour, seasoned with salt and pepper. Fry the meat over a high heat until nicely browned.

3 Heat the butter in a large heavy-based saucepan and gently fry the onion for about 5 minutes, until soft. Add the remaining flour and tomato purée, and stir over a low heat for a minute. Slowly add the marinade, stirring constantly to avoid lumps forming. Bring to the boil and simmer until reduced by half.

4 Add the beef stock and the pieces of beef. Bring back to a simmer, cover with a lid and simmer very gently for about 2–2½ hours, until the meat is tender. It's difficult to put an exact time on braised meats, sometimes an extra half an hour may be required. The best way to check is by tasting the meat.

5 Once the meat is cooked, the sauce should have thickened to a gravy-like consistency; if not, mix a little cornflour to a paste with some water, stir into the sauce and simmer for a few minutes. Adjust the seasoning if necessary and serve.

shepherd's pie

Good quality minced meat will make all the difference to your shepherd's pie; don't be tempted by the low priced, special-offer mince on the shelves for this recipe.

SERVES 4

450g (1lb) good quality coarse lamb mince

450g (1lb) good quality coarse beef mince

2 tablespoons vegetable oil

500g (1lb 2oz) onions, peeled and finely chopped

2 garlic cloves, peeled and crushed

1 teaspoon chopped thyme leaves

1 tablespoon plain flour

1 tablespoon tomato purée

glass of red wine

1 tablespoon Worcestershire sauce

1 litre (1¾ pints) beef stock

salt and freshly ground black pepper

FOR THE TOPPING:

500g (1lb 2oz) potatoes, peeled and quartered

25g (1oz) butter

a little milk

200g (7oz) parsnips, peeled, cored and roughly chopped

1 Season the minced meat with salt and pepper. Heat a little oil in a frying pan until it is almost smoking and cook the meat in small batches for a few minutes, turning with a wooden spoon, until well coloured, then drain in a colander to remove the fat.

2 Heat a little more oil in a heavy-based pan and gently fry the onions with the garlic and thyme until very soft. Add the meat, dust it with the flour and then add the tomato purée. Cook for a few minutes, stirring constantly. Slowly stir in the wine, Worcestershire sauce and beef stock. Bring to the boil, lower the heat and simmer for about 45–50 minutes until the liquid has thickened. Adjust the seasoning and set aside to cool.

3 Meanwhile, cook the potatoes in boiling salted water for about 15 minutes, until tender. Drain and return to the pan over a low heat for a minute or so to dry. Mash the potatoes, season well, then add the butter and a dash of milk to give a firm mash.

4 While the potatoes are cooking, cook the parsnips in boiling salted water for about 10–12 minutes until they are soft. Drain in a colander, then return to the pan over a low heat for a minute or so to drive off any excess moisture. Purée the parsnips in a food processor or mash them smoothly with a potato masher and mix them with the mashed potato. Season.

5 Preheat the oven to 200°C (fan oven 180°C), gas mark 6. Put the meat into a large serving dish or individual dishes and top with the potato mixture, spooning it on evenly and roughing up the surface with a fork. Bake for 35–40 minutes until the topping is golden.

Cornish pasties

Cornwall's famous pasties were originally made for miners, fishermen, farmers and children to take to work or school, though fillings would vary depending on the wealth of the household. Some would only contain swede, potato and onion, plus some leek, and perhaps ham off-cuts.

MAKES 6–8

FOR THE PASTRY:
500g (1lb 2oz) plain flour
2 teaspoons salt
125g (4½oz) butter, chilled and diced
125g (4½oz) lard, chilled and diced
a little milk, to mix
1 medium egg, beaten, to seal and glaze

FOR THE FILLING:
200g (7oz) swede, peeled
200g (7oz) large potatoes, peeled
250ml (8fl oz) beef stock
500g (1lb 2oz) rump or frying steak
1 tablespoon vegetable oil
1 large onion, peeled and finely chopped
1 tablespoon Worcestershire sauce
1 teaspoon chopped thyme leaves
salt and freshly ground black pepper

1 To make the filling, cut the swede and potatoes roughly into 2cm (¾ inch) pieces and cook separately in boiling salted water until just tender. Drain and leave to cool. Meanwhile, boil the beef stock in a pan to reduce right down to 2–3 tablespoons. Trim any fat from the steak, then cut into 5mm (¼ inch) pieces, or coarsely mince.

2 Heat the oil in a large heavy-based pan and gently cook the onion until translucent, then add the meat and cook over a high heat, turning, until evenly browned. Add the stock, Worcestershire sauce, thyme leaves and some seasoning, and cook over a medium heat until the stock has almost totally reduced. Set aside to cool.

3 To make the pastry, mix the flour and salt together, then rub in the butter and lard with your fingers, or using a food processor, until the texture of fine breadcrumbs. Mix in enough milk to give a smooth dough which leaves the sides of the bowl clean.

4 Roll out the pastry on a lightly floured board to a 3mm (⅛ inch) thickness and cut out 6 circles, about 18cm (7 inches) in diameter, using a plate or bowl as a template.

5 Add the vegetables to the cooled meat, mix well and adjust the seasoning. Spoon the filling evenly along the middle of the pastry discs, then brush around the edges with beaten egg. Bring the edges of the pastry up over the filling and crimp the edges together with your fingers. Brush with beaten egg and cut a small slit in the top for steam to escape. Chill for about 30 minutes. Meanwhile, preheat the oven to 200°C (fan oven 180°C), gas mark 6.

6 Bake the pasties for 20 minutes, then turn the oven down to 180°C (fan oven 160°C), gas mark 4 and cook them for another 20 minutes or so until golden. If the pasties are browning too fast in the oven, cover them with foil or greaseproof paper.

boiled meats

The term 'boiled meat' is something of a misnomer, as the meat is simmered with flavourings very gently to ensure it doesn't toughen. This traditional technique is applied to various meats and provides a delicious alternative to ready-cooked meats.

Home-cooked ham is really quite simple, and full of flavour. It's the sort of joint you can enjoy and afterwards use leftovers cold for sandwiches and salads, with the bonus of stock for soup and dishes like pease pudding (page 143). Any cut of ham – hock, gammon or a boiling and roasting joint off the shelf – will do. Some joints are saltier than others so, to be on the safe side, soak in cold water overnight.

Cooked with vegetables and herbs, salt beef is light, delicious, and creates the most flavoursome stock and serving liquor. Salt beef usually comes as brisket or silverside, often pre-packed with cooking instructions. Leftovers make great sandwiches.

▼ **boiled ham**

To serve 4, first soak 4 unsmoked ham hocks, each 300–400g (11–14oz), or a 1kg (2¼lb), boned ham or bacon joint in water overnight to remove excess salt. Next day, drain and rinse in cold water. Put in a large pan with 4 small onions, 2 halved carrots, 1 bay leaf, 3 cloves, a few thyme sprigs and 1 tsp black peppercorns. Cover with cold water, bring to the boil and simmer for 3 hours. Remove the ham, reserving the

cooking liquor, and leave to cool. Once the ham is cool enough to handle, remove and discard the fat from the hocks, then carefully remove the outer section of meat and the large bone, leaving the small bone attached to the central eye of meat. Alternatively, if you are using a ham joint, just remove the string and carve into thick slices. Serve with the onions and carrots if you like, and coat with the parsley sauce (right). Accompany with mash or colcannon (page 138).

horseradish dumplings

Make these to serve with boiled salt beef (right). Sift 125g (4oz) plain flour and 1 tsp baking powder into a bowl; add ½ tsp salt. Mix in 65g (2½oz) suet, 1 tbsp chopped parsley and 1 tbsp freshly grated horseradish, then add enough water to form a sticky dough. Flour your hands and roll the dough into 12 balls. When the cooked beef has been removed from the pan, poach the dumplings in the cooking liquid for 15 minutes.

▼ ## boiled salt beef with carrots and dumplings

To serve 4, first soak a 1kg (2¼lb) joint of salted silverside or brisket overnight. Next day, drain and rinse in cold water, then put into a large saucepan with 4 small onions, 12 small carrots, 3 cloves, 10 black peppercorns, 2 mace blades, 1 bay leaf and a few thyme sprigs. Add enough water to cover the beef by about 6cm (2½ inches) and bring to the boil. Simmer gently, covered, for about 2½–3 hours until tender, removing the

parsley sauce

Make this to serve with boiled ham (left). Melt 25g (1oz) butter in a heavy-based pan and gently cook 2 finely chopped shallots until soft. Add 25g (1oz) flour and 1 tsp English mustard; stir well. Gradually stir in 150ml (¼ pint) milk mixed with 150ml (¼ pint) of the ham cooking liquid. Bring to the boil, season and simmer for about 20 minutes until quite thick, stirring occasionally. Add 2 tbsp double cream and 2 tbsp chopped parsley, adjust the seasoning and simmer for another minute.

carrots and onions as soon as they are cooked; set aside. Remove the cooked beef from the pan and keep warm.

Poach the dumplings in the liquor (see above left) then remove and strain the liquid through a fine sieve. Return to the pan and boil to reduce by about half, until it has a good strong flavour. Skim off any fat. To serve, reheat the onions, carrots and dumplings in the reduced liquor. Slice the beef and serve in deep plates with the carrots, onions and dumplings, spooning over the liquid.

roast pork with crackling and Bramley apple sauce

Getting the crackling on roast pork right isn't as difficult as people think. Although getting the cooking of the pork right in conjunction with crisp crackling is more of an issue, especially with smaller cuts. Loin with crackling is a nice cut, but you will need to remove the skin and cook it separately or the meat will be overcooked. I actually prefer boned and rolled shoulder and leg joints, as they have more flavour and the crackling can be left on all the way through cooking.

SERVES 4–6

1 boned and rolled joint of pork (see above), about 1–1.5kg (2¼–3¼lb)

olive oil, to brush

1–2 onions, peeled and cut into chunks

3–4 carrots, peeled and cut into chunks

sea salt

FOR THE GRAVY:

½ tablespoon flour

½ glass of red or white wine

500ml (16fl oz) beef stock

FOR THE BRAMLEY APPLE SAUCE:

good knob of butter

650g (1lb 7oz) Bramley apples, peeled, cored and cut into chunks

50g (2oz) light brown sugar, or to taste

1 If it hasn't been done already, score the skin of the joint with a very sharp knife at about 5mm–1cm (¼–½ inch) intervals, cutting right through to the fat. Rub some sea salt and olive oil over the skin and leave to stand at room temperature for about 45 minutes. Alternatively, you can pour boiling water over the skin, which scalds it and helps to crisp it up, then proceed as above.

2 Preheat the oven to 200°C (fan oven 180°C), gas mark 6. Heat a roasting tin in the oven, then add the pork with the onions and carrots. Roast in the oven for about 1½ hours, basting the joint every so often. If the pork appears to be browning too rapidly, the oven may need to be turned down slightly.

3 When the pork is cooked through, remove it from the roasting tin and leave to rest on a plate. Don't be tempted to cover the pork with foil as the steam will make the crackling go soft (the crackling itself functions like a cover and keeps the heat in the meat). If the crackling isn't crisp, you can always cut it from the meat and finish it in the oven.

4 For the gravy, dust the vegetables in the roasting tin with the flour and cook over a low heat on the hob for 2 minutes. Add the wine and stock, and simmer for a few minutes, scraping up any residue from the bottom of the pan with a wooden spoon. Transfer to a saucepan and simmer for 20 minutes.

5 Meanwhile, make the apple sauce. Melt the butter in a frying pan and sauté the apples with a third of the sugar for about 5 minutes, until nicely coloured and beginning to break down. Continuing to stir, add the rest of the sugar (to taste) and cook for a few more minutes, until the apples are broken down but not completely puréed.

6 Strain the gravy through a fine sieve into a jug. To serve, slice the pork through the crackling. Pour some hot gravy over each plateful of meat and serve the rest on the side, with the apple sauce.

roast lamb with mint jelly and lavender

Lavender, like rosemary, gives an amazing aroma to lamb as it roasts and, with the mint jelly as an accompaniment, leaves that summery feel on your tongue. It's up to you which cut you use, but best end (rack) is always tender, looks terrific and carves easily. Make the mint jelly several days in advance for convenience. You'll have more than you need here but it's really not worth making a small amount, and it will keep for a few months in the fridge in sterilised jars.
Illustrated on previous page

SERVES 4

2 best ends (racks) of lamb, French trimmed,
   each 400–450g (14oz–1lb)
few sprigs of lavender
1 garlic clove, peeled and thinly sliced
1 tablespoon vegetable oil
sea salt and freshly ground black pepper
pan gravy (page 87), optional, to serve

FOR THE MINT JELLY:

2kg (4½lb) cooking apples
300ml (½ pint) cider vinegar
25g (1oz) mint leaves
about 300g (11oz) preserving or
   granulated sugar
10 sheets leaf gelatine

1   Make the mint jelly at least 2 days ahead. Roughly chop the apples, including the peel and cores. Place in a heavy-based saucepan with 1 litre (1¾ pints) water, bring to the boil and simmer very gently for 40 minutes. Add the vinegar and continue cooking for 5 minutes. You'll need a jelly bag and stand, or a stainless steel or plastic colander lined with 3 layers of muslin and set over a bowl. Tip the contents of the pan into the jelly bag or lined colander and allow to drip through for about 4 hours or overnight.

2   Bring a small pan of water to the boil and dip the mint leaves in for 2 seconds only. Drain in a sieve, refresh under cold running water, then dry on kitchen paper. Finely chop the leaves and put to one side.

3   Measure the apple liquid and add 100g (3½oz) sugar for every 100ml (3½fl oz). Pour the liquid into a saucepan, add the sugar and stir over a low heat until dissolved. Bring to the boil and boil for 5 minutes. Meanwhile, soak the gelatine leaves in cold water to cover for a few minutes to soften, then squeeze out excess liquid. Remove the apple syrup from the heat, add the gelatine, stirring to dissolve, then stir in the mint. Pour into sterilised Kilner jars, seal and store in a cool dark place, or refrigerate.

4   When ready to cook the lamb, preheat the oven to 220°C (fan oven 200°C), gas mark 7. With a small sharp knife, make 8–10 incisions in the fat covering the lamb, about 1cm (½ inch) deep. Put a tiny sprig of lavender and a slice of garlic into each slit and season the lamb with salt and pepper.

5   Spoon the oil into a shallow roasting tin and heat in the oven for about 5 minutes. Put the lamb in the roasting tin, fat side down, and roast for 15 minutes, then turn the lamb over and cook for another 15 minutes for pink meat; leave it for another 10 minutes for medium; 15 minutes for well done.

6   Transfer the lamb to a warmed plate and rest in a warm place for 5 minutes while you make a gravy with the pan juices. Carve the lamb in between the bones and serve with the mint jelly and gravy.

leg of lamb with caper sauce

Mutton would traditionally have been used for this dish, but you rarely find it these days. Lamb works well, though it won't deliver quite the same intensity of flavour.

SERVES 4

1 boned and rolled leg of lamb, about 800g–1kg
  (1³⁄₄–2¹⁄₄lb)
2 onions, peeled and halved
1 leek, trimmed, roughly chopped and rinsed
few thyme sprigs
1 bay leaf
10 black peppercorns
600ml (1 pint) chicken stock
1 teaspoon salt

FOR THE CAPER SAUCE:

25g (1oz) butter
25g (1oz) plain flour
100ml (3¹⁄₂fl oz) double cream
100g (3¹⁄₂oz) capers, rinsed in cold water
1 tablespoon chopped parsley
salt and freshly ground black pepper

1 Put the lamb into a saucepan into which it just fits and add the onions, leek, thyme, bay leaf and peppercorns. Mix the chicken stock with an equal quantity of water and pour into the pan to cover the meat. (If necessary, add a little more water or dilute stock). Add the salt and bring to the boil. Skim off any scum from the surface, lower the heat and simmer for 1¹⁄₂ hours. Pour 500ml (16fl oz) of the stock into a jug (for the sauce) and leave the lamb in the rest of the liquor, covered with a lid, until required.

2 To make the sauce, melt the butter in a heavy-based pan, add the flour and stir well. Gradually stir in the stock and bring to the boil. Remove the cooked onions from the lamb cooking liquor and add them to the sauce. Simmer for 30 minutes over a low heat.

3 Transfer the sauce to a blender or food processor and whiz until smooth, then pass through a fine sieve into a clean pan. Add the cream and simmer until the sauce has thickened to a coating consistency. Add the capers and parsley, and season with salt and pepper to taste.

4 Remove the lamb from the cooking liquid and place on a board. Remove any string and cut the lamb into 5mm–1cm (¹⁄₄–¹⁄₂ inch) thick slices. Arrange on warm plates and serve with the caper sauce.

Barnsley chops with baked shallots and parsley

Less familiar then ordinary loin chops and cutlets, the Barnsley chop is actually a double loin chop cut across the saddle and is sometimes simply called a saddle chop. The story goes that it originated in the Kings Head pub in Barnsley in 1849 to provide a substantial lunch for farmers. Cut to generous proportions, these chops were also served at the celebration of the opening of Barnsley Town Hall in 1933. Obviously, if you can't find Barnsley chops, just use two good ordinary loin chops per person.

SERVES 4

500g (1lb 2oz) shallots, unpeeled
4 Barnsley chops (see above), each about
  200g (7oz)
100ml (3½fl oz) lamb or beef stock
good knob of unsalted butter
1 tablespoon chopped parsley
sea salt and freshly ground black pepper

1 Preheat the oven to 200°C (fan oven 180°C), gas mark 6. Put the shallots, still in their skins, on a roasting tin and bake for 45 minutes. Leave them to cool, then top and tail them with a sharp knife and gently squeeze the onions out their skins.

2 When the shallots are almost cooked, heat a lightly oiled griddle pan or the grill to its hottest setting. Season the chops with salt and pepper, and grill for 4–5 minutes on each side for pink, or 7–8 minutes for medium.

3 While the chops are cooking, put the shallots into a frying pan with the stock and cook over a high heat to reduce the stock until it is almost totally evaporated. Add the butter and chopped parsley, lightly season with salt and pepper, and stir until the butter has melted into the liquid to form a glaze.

4 Place the chops on warm plates. Spoon the glazed shallots on top, or serve them separately.

Lancashire hot pot

This is one of the best known dishes in the North of England. There are various versions of Lancashire hot pot, but the main ingredients are a flavoursome cut of lamb, such as neck chops, and potatoes. Kidneys – and even black pudding – can be added along with the potatoes and onions. Back in the days when they were cheap, a few oysters would be put under the potato.

SERVES 4

800g (1¾lb) lamb neck fillet
6 lambs' kidneys, halved and trimmed (optional)
flour, to dust
4–5 tablespoons vegetable oil
500g (1lb 2oz) onions, peeled and thinly sliced

65g (2½oz) unsalted butter, plus extra to brush
800ml (1⅓ pints) lamb or beef stock
1 teaspoon chopped rosemary leaves
1 kg (2¼lb) large potatoes, peeled and thinly sliced
salt and freshly ground black pepper

1   Preheat the oven to 220°C (fan oven 200°C), gas mark 7. Cut the lamb roughly into 3–4cm (1¼–1½ inch) chunks, season with salt and pepper and dust with flour. Season and lightly flour the kidneys if using, keeping them separate.

2   Heat 2 tablespoons oil in a heavy-based frying pan and fry the lamb, a few pieces at a time, over a high heat until nicely coloured. Drain in a colander. Fry and drain the kidneys in the same way, then mix with the lamb and set aside.

3   Wipe the pan clean. Heat another 2 tablespoons oil in the pan and fry the onions over a high heat until they begin to colour. Add the butter and continue to cook for a few minutes until the onions soften. Dust them with a tablespoon of flour, stir well, then gradually add the stock, stirring to avoid lumps. Sprinkle in the chopped rosemary. Bring to the boil, season with salt and pepper and simmer for about 10 minutes.

4   Now you're ready to assemble the pot. Cover the bottom of a casserole dish with a layer of potatoes, then add a layer of meat with a little sauce, then another layer of potatoes. Continue until the meat has all been used. Finish the top with a layer of nicely overlapping potato slices.

5   Brush the top layer of potatoes with a little of the sauce. Cover and cook in the oven for about 30 minutes, then turn the oven down to 140°C (fan oven 120°C), gas mark 1 and cook for a further 2 hours.

6   Remove the lid from the pot and turn the oven back up to 220°C (fan oven 200°C), gas mark 7. Brush the top with a little melted butter and cook, uncovered, for a further 15–20 minutes to brown the potatoes.

Irish stew

There is much discussion about the correct ingredients for an Irish stew. However, a simple dish like this, which was probably originally cooked in a three-legged pot on the open fire, must surely have used only the ingredients that were available on the land. No supermarkets to trawl around then, looking for baby vegetables and fresh thyme. A cut like neck of lamb withstands long cooking, remains moist and gives the broth the perfect depth of natural flavour. Lamb or mutton neck chops are traditional, but neck fillet is readily available these days and rather more user-friendly. Some versions have every vegetable imaginable, which just makes it into yet another meat and vegetable stew.

SERVES 4–6

600–700g (1¼–1½lb) lamb neck fillet
1 litre (1¾ pints) lamb stock
1 teaspoon chopped thyme leaves
500g (1lb 2oz) large button onions, or small
  onions about the size of a squash ball, peeled
700g (1½lb) small baking potatoes, or large
  new potatoes (same size as onions), peeled
salt and freshly ground black pepper

1 Cut the lamb into 4cm (1½ inch) chunks and put into a heavy-based pan with the stock and thyme leaves. Season with salt and pepper and bring to the boil. Lower the heat and simmer for 30 minutes.

2 Add the onions to the pan and simmer for another 20 minutes. Meanwhile, preheat the oven to 180°C (fan oven 160°C), gas mark 4.

3 Transfer the contents of the pan to an ovenproof dish, stir in the potatoes and cover with a lid. Cook in the oven for 1 hour, or a little longer if the lamb is not soft. Depending on the time of year, the lamb can be a little tougher and will take more cooking.

devilled lambs' kidneys

This makes a good breakfast or brunch dish, as well as a light main course. Always try to buy fresh lambs' kidneys, as they will have a better texture when cooked than frozen ones.

SERVES 4

20 lambs' kidneys, halved and trimmed
  of sinews
1–2 tablespoons vegetable oil
good knob of butter
3 shallots, peeled and finely chopped
1 garlic clove, peeled and crushed
2 tablespoons cider vinegar
2 teaspoons English mustard
2 teaspoons tomato ketchup
100ml (3½fl oz) pan gravy (page 87), or
  basic gravy (page 88)
1 tablespoon chopped parsley
sea salt and cayenne pepper
4 thick slices of buttered toast, to serve

1   Heat a frying pan until almost smoking. Season the kidneys with salt and cayenne pepper and fry them in a little vegetable oil for 2 minutes over a high heat until coloured but still pink. Transfer them to a plate.

2   Melt the butter in a saucepan, add the shallots and garlic, and cook gently for a couple of minutes until soft. Add the cider vinegar, mustard and ketchup, and simmer for a minute. Add the gravy and parsley, bring to the boil and simmer for a couple of minutes until the sauce is thick.

3   Add the kidneys to the pan and simmer for 30 seconds to reheat them. Spoon on to hot buttered toast and serve straightaway.

6 vegetables

peas with bacon and onions

This dish is similar to the French *petits pois bonne femme*. If you are used just to plain old boiled peas, you'll find that bacon and spring onions give them a new lease of life. Use fresh peas when they are in season – you'll need about 1kg (2¼lb) peas in the pod to give this shelled weight. *Illustrated left*

SERVES 4

125g (4oz) slices of rindless streaky bacon
75g (3oz) butter
400g (14oz) shelled fresh or frozen peas

2 teaspoons sugar
1 bunch of spring onions (preferably the
 bulbous ones)
sea salt and freshly ground black pepper

1 Cut the bacon into 1cm (½ inch) dice. Melt 25g (1oz) butter in a pan and gently cook the bacon over a low heat for 3–4 minutes without allowing it to colour.

2 Meanwhile, put the peas into a saucepan and just cover them with boiling water. Add 25g (1oz) of the remaining butter, season well and add the sugar. Bring back to the boil and cook over a medium heat for 6–7 minutes (2 minutes only for frozen) or until tender. Drain in a colander set over a bowl to save the liquid.

3 Cut the spring onions into 2.5cm (1 inch) lengths, put into the empty pan and pour just enough of the reserved liquid over to cover them. Boil rapidly until most of the liquid has evaporated, then add the rest of the butter and mix with the peas and the bacon. Check the seasoning and serve.

buttered greens with Kentish cob nuts

Kentish cob nuts are available during the autumn months. They give a nice texture to greens which can otherwise be a bit boring on their own. If you have missed the cob nut season, then chestnuts make a good alternative.

SERVES 4

1kg (2¼lb) spring greens or Savoy cabbage,
 trimmed and stalk removed

100g (3½oz) shelled cob nuts
65g (2½oz) butter
sea salt and freshly ground black pepper

1 Cut the spring greens or cabbage roughly into 3cm (1¼ inch) squares. Cook in plenty of boiling salted water for 4–5 minutes until tender, then drain in a colander.

2 Meanwhile, preheat the grill to medium. Roughly chop the cob nuts and toast lightly. Drain the greens well and toss with the toasted nuts and butter. Season with salt and pepper, then serve.

creamed Brussels sprouts

This is a simple way to use up leftover Brussels sprouts, or you can prepare them from fresh. Serve as an accompaniment to poultry and game dishes.
Illustrated right

SERVES 4–6
500g (1lb 2oz) large Brussels sprouts
150ml (¼ pint) double cream
50g (2oz) butter
sea salt and freshly ground black pepper

1 Cook the sprouts in boiling salted water for 5–10 minutes until just tender, then drain well and allow to cool slightly. Slice the sprouts thinly.

2 Boil the cream to reduce by half, then add the sprouts and season with salt and pepper. Simmer for 4–5 minutes over a low heat, stirring every so often. Add the butter and serve.

buttered samphire

Marsh samphire, or sea asparagus, can be found on the salt marshes around the coast during the summer months. It has a natural salty taste of the sea, which makes it a perfect accompaniment for fish. In East Anglia, you'll find it on menus, steamed and served with melted butter as a starter.

SERVES 4
300–400g (11–14oz) samphire, woody
   stalks trimmed
melted butter (as much as you like)
freshly ground black pepper

1 Cook the samphire in boiling unsalted water (or steam it if you prefer) for 2–3 minutes until tender. Drain thoroughly in a colander.

2 Toss the samphire with melted butter and black pepper to taste, then serve straightaway.

turnips with chervil

Prepared and cooked in the right way, turnips, swede and parsnips are the best of the root vegetables. I cannot think why they are dismissed as cattle fodder by some, especially in France.
Illustrated on previous page

SERVES 4
800g (1³/₄lb) young turnips, peeled
2 teaspoons sugar

100g (3¹/₂oz) butter
1 tablespoon chopped chervil
sea salt and freshly ground black pepper

1   If the turnips are very small leave them whole, otherwise quarter them. Put the turnips into a pan and just cover with boiling water. Add the sugar and half of the butter, and season generously with salt and pepper. Bring back to the boil and cook over a medium heat for 7–8 minutes or until tender.

2   Drain the turnips in a colander, then toss with the remaining butter and chopped chervil. Taste and adjust the seasoning, then serve.

honey-roasted parsnips

This is the perfect accompaniment to a roast joint. Lots of people don't like parsnips for some reason and, as I've mentioned above, in some countries they are fed to cattle. What a waste – they have a delicious natural fluffy texture and sweet flavour. I'm sure the cows think the same.

SERVES 4–6
700–800g (1¹/₂–1³/₄lb) parsnips
65–75g (2¹/₂–3oz) beef dripping
2 tablespoons thin honey
sea salt and freshly ground black pepper

1   Top and tail the parsnips. If the skins are clean they don't need to be peeled, otherwise peel them. Quarter the parsnips lengthways and remove the hard core which runs down the centre. Cook the parsnip quarters in boiling salted water for 5 minutes, drain in a colander and leave to cool.

2   Preheat the oven to 200°C (fan oven 180°C), gas mark 6 and heat a roasting tray in the oven. Melt the beef dripping in the hot tray, then add the parsnips and season with salt and pepper. Roast for about 30 minutes, turning occasionally, until the parsnips are nicely coloured. (Alternatively, they can be roasted around a joint of meat.)

3   Add the honey, turn the parsnips to coat and return the tray to the oven for a further 5 minutes, basting once or twice with the honey and dripping until they are golden. Serve immediately.

roasted marrow with garlic and herbs

Have we been put off by marrow because it's been served up to us without passion or understanding? Like its cousins in the pumpkin and squash family, marrows are looked at with interest by prospective buyers but rarely find their way into the shopping trolley. Perhaps their size and shape are rather daunting and they look difficult to tackle. Try to choose young marrows, as these have the best flavour and their skin can be left on.

SERVES 4

1 young marrow, about 1kg (2¼lb)
1 tablespoon olive oil
2 teaspoons chopped thyme leaves
4 garlic cloves, peeled and crushed
65g (2½oz) butter
2 tablespoons chopped parsley
sea salt and freshly ground black pepper

1 Cut the marrow into quarters lengthways and scoop out the seeds with a spoon. Cut the flesh into 2cm (¾ inch) thick slices, lay them on a tray and season well with salt and pepper. Leave to stand for 30 minutes. Preheat the oven to 230°C (fan oven 210°C), gas mark 8.

2 Heat the olive oil in a roasting tray in the oven for 5 minutes. Add the marrow slices and sprinkle with the chopped thyme. Roast for 15 minutes, turning occasionally, then add the garlic and cook for a further 5–10 minutes, until the marrow is nicely browned.

3 To serve, toss the roasted marrow with the butter and chopped parsley.

roasted beets with horseradish

There are other ways to treat beetroot, apart from pickling. It makes a delicious soup, is good in salads and can be cooked simply to serve as an accompaniment. Beetroot is an easy vegetable to cook, although a bit messy to peel. If you can't get a hold of fresh horseradish, then the grated horseradish sold in jars will work well.

SERVES 4

1kg (2¼lb) small beetroot
1–2 tablespoons olive oil
few thyme sprigs

65g (2½oz) freshly grated horseradish
knob of butter
sea salt and freshly ground black pepper

1 Cook the beetroot in their skins in a pan of boiling salted water for about 1 hour, or until they are tender to the point of a knife. Drain in a colander and leave to cool. Preheat the oven to 200°C (fan oven 180°C), gas mark 6.

2 Wearing rubber gloves to avoid staining your hands, remove the skin from the beetroot and trim the ends if necessary. If the beetroot are very small leave them whole, otherwise cut into quarters.

3 Heat the olive oil in a roasting tray in the oven for about 5 minutes. Add the beetroot and season with salt and pepper. Cook for 30 minutes, then scatter over the thyme leaves and continue cooking for another 15–20 minutes until nicely coloured.

4 Scatter the horseradish over the beetroot, add the butter and turn to coat, then return to the oven for 10 minutes. Serve hot.

mash

With so many varieties of potato on the market, choosing one with a good flavour and texture for mashing can be a challenge. Packet and shelf guidelines suggest uses, but it helps to get to know your spuds. King Edwards are my favourite all-round potato. A while ago, we discovered that by baking these floury potatoes, then scooping out and mashing the flesh, you ended up with a consistent, well flavoured, earthy mash that would take a good amount of milk, cream or butter.

An old fashioned hand-held masher is adequate for mashing, but a potato ricer is an invaluable tool. It's a bit like a large garlic crusher and it gets the potatoes nice and fine before you add the butter and milk or cream. Well flavoured potatoes need just a touch of milk, as cream will make them heavy, and you certainly won't need cream if you are serving mash with something as rich as braised beef or duck.

▲ colcannon

Closely related to champ (right), colcannon comprises mashed potatoes and cabbage or kale, sometimes with the addition of spring onions. It came to England from Ireland in the 18th century, and became a favourite of the upper classes, because it is a perfect match for rich stews and boiled meats. To make colcannon, simply make a quantity of mash as above and mix with a large bunch of chopped, blanched spring onions and 350g (12oz) chopped well cooked cabbage, such as Savoy.

▼ simple mash

To serve 4, put 1kg (2¼lb) peeled, quartered floury potatoes in a saucepan, cover well with cold water and add salt. Bring to the boil and simmer for about 15 minutes until tender. Drain and return to the pan over a low heat for a minute or so to dry out. Put through a potato ricer, or mash by hand. Season well, add 50g (2oz) butter, then stir in milk or double cream to taste (don't lose the earthy flavour). Check the seasoning.

▼ bubble and squeak

This is traditionally made with leftovers but, of course, you can use freshly cooked vegetables. To serve 4–6, combine 150g (5oz) chopped cooked swede, 250g (9oz) chopped cooked cabbage, 250g (9oz) chopped cooked Brussels sprouts, 1 chopped cooked leek and 250g (9oz) quartered cooked Charlotte or other waxy potatoes, in a bowl and mix well. Season with salt, pepper, celery salt and Worcestershire sauce

champ

Champ is Irish in origin and consists of mashed potato and spring onions. It has been called various names, such as pandy, cally and poundy. Champ was prepared particularly for Hallowe'en when cauldrons of potatoes were boiled and pounded – probably where the name 'poundy' came from. To make champ, simply make a quantity of mash as above and mix with a large bunch of chopped, blanched spring onions.

to taste. Heat a little oil in a non-stick frying pan until almost smoking and fry the mixture a little at a time, turning, until it begins to colour. Then return to the bowl and leave to cool. Adjust the seasoning, mould the cooled mixture into even-sized cakes and refrigerate. When ready to serve, lightly flour the cakes and fry in a little oil for about 3–4 minutes on each side until golden brown. Serve as an accompaniment, or topped with a fried egg for brunch.

pan haggerty

This dish seem to appear in different guises all over the world, like *pommes Anna* and the various French potato gratins and Welsh onion cake (page 142). I've even had a similar dish in Spain that was thinner, so it was pizza-like, and topped with diced bacon and herbs. I suppose when you have simple ingredients from the land, like potatoes and onions, you need to be creative with them. An ovenproof frying pan is useful here, otherwise use a non-stick pan and transfer the potato cake to a baking tray to finish cooking in the oven.

SERVES 4

500g (1lb 2oz) large potatoes
40g (1½oz) butter
250g (9oz) onions, peeled and thinly sliced

75g (3oz) beef dripping
125g (4oz) mature Cheddar cheese, grated
sea salt and freshly ground black pepper

1 Preheat the oven to 190°C (fan oven 170°C), gas mark 5. Peel and thinly slice the potatoes on a mandolin, or the slicer on the side of a cheese grater. Melt the butter in a pan and gently cook the onions over a medium heat for about 10 minutes until they soften.

2 Heat half of the dripping in heavy-based frying pan (preferably ovenproof and ideally non-stick). Remove from the heat and arrange a layer of the sliced potatoes in the pan, then build up layers of onions, cheese and potatoes, seasoning the layers and finishing with a layer of potatoes.

3 Return the pan to a medium heat and fry until the bottom layer begins to colour. Put the rest of the dripping on top of the potatoes then put the pan into the oven. (If your frying pan isn't ovenproof, then slide the potato 'cake' on to a baking tray.)

4 Bake for 45 minutes until golden brown, increasing the temperature to 220°C (fan oven 200°C), gas mark 7 for the last 10 minutes to brown the top if necessary. Loosen the sides of the potato cake with a palette knife and carefully invert on to a large warm plate to serve.

roast potatoes with goose fat

Goose fat gives roast potatoes that rich luxury taste. If you can't find goose or duck fat, then bought or leftover beef dripping from a roasted joint of meat will give you a close result.

SERVES 4

1.5kg (3¼lb) King Edwards or similar potatoes,
  peeled and halved or quartered if large
150g (5oz) goose or duck fat
sea salt and freshly ground black pepper

1 Par-cook the potatoes in boiling salted water for 10 minutes. Drain and return to the pan over a low heat for a minute or so to drive off excess moisture. Turn off the heat, put the lid on and leave for 5 minutes, then give the pan a brief shake and leave them for another 15 minutes. This will steam the potatoes through and rough up the edges a bit, which gives them that nice crisp skin and allows the goose fat to be absorbed by the potato. Preheat the oven to 220°C (fan oven 200°C), gas mark 7.

2 Put the goose fat in a roasting tray and preheat in the oven. Season the potatoes with salt and pepper, then add to the tray and roll them in the hot goose fat. Roast for about 45 minutes until crisp, basting every 15 minutes or so. Serve straightaway.

Welsh onion cake

Known in Welsh as *teisen nionod*, this is a bit like the famous French *pommes boulanger*, which is cooked in meat stock. If you are roasting a joint of meat, you can finish cooking it on a trivet over the onion cake so that the juices get absorbed into the potatoes and onions.

SERVES 4–6

800g (1¾lb) large potatoes
100g (3½oz) butter, melted, plus extra to brush
500g (1lb 2oz) onions, peeled and sliced
sea salt and freshly ground black pepper

1 Preheat the oven to 200°C (fan oven 180°C), gas mark 6. Peel and thinly slice the potatoes, then rinse briefly in water and pat dry on a clean tea towel. Put them a bowl, season with salt and pepper, and mix with the melted butter.

2 Butter a shallow ovenproof serving dish and layer the potatoes and onions alternately, beginning with the potato slices and finishing with a neat layer of overlapped potato slices on top. Cover with foil or a lid and bake for 1 hour. Brush with a little more butter and cook uncovered for a further 15–20 minutes to brown the top. Serve hot.

pease pudding

Traditionally this Northern dish would be made by tying the dried peas in a muslin cloth and boiling them with a ham joint. If you have prepared a boiled ham (on page 112), don't throw the stock away – use it here, or cook the two together. You can flake any pieces of cooked ham into the pudding for a bit of added texture. You'll probably need to soak the split peas overnight in cold water to cover, but check the packet first as some of the pulses on sale these days don't need lengthy soaking.

SERVES 4

450g (1lb) dried yellow split peas
about 1 litre (1³/₄ pints) ham stock (page 113)
  or chicken stock
1 medium egg, beaten
65g (2¹/₂oz) butter, plus extra to grease
sea salt and freshly ground black pepper

1 Soak the dried split peas in cold water to cover overnight, then drain and rinse.

2 Drain the soaked split peas and place in a large pan. Add ham or chicken stock to cover them generously and simmer for 1 hour or so, until tender. Drain and tip into a large bowl.

3 Add the egg and butter to the peas and mix well, seasoning with salt and pepper. Transfer to a greased 1.2 litre (2 pint) pudding basin and cover the top with a sheet of foil, pleated in the centre. Secure under the rim with string.

4 Put the pudding basin into a steamer or saucepan containing enough boiling water to come halfway up the side of the basin and steam for 1 hour. Check the water level during cooking as you may have to top it up with more boiling water. Alternatively, you can cook it in a deep-roasting tin half-filled with boiling water in the oven at 180°C (fan oven 160°C), gas mark 4 for 1 hour.

5 Lift the pudding basin from the pan, remove the foil and run a knife around the side of the pudding to loosen it. Turn out on to a warm plate and serve.

7 puddings

rhubarb syllabub

Rhubarb is available from early February for a few months, but you can use other fruits in season, such as raspberries, plums and exotic fruits, like passion fruit.

Illustrated left

SERVES 4

250g (9oz) young rhubarb, trimmed and cut into
  2cm (³/4 inch) pieces
150g (5oz) caster sugar
3 tablespoons grenadine syrup

FOR THE SYLLABUB:
400ml (14fl oz) double cream
100g (3¹/2oz) caster sugar
juice of 1 small lemon
small glass of sherry or sweet wine

1 Cook the rhubarb with the sugar and grenadine in a covered pan over a medium heat, stirring occasionally, until soft, about 10 minutes. Tip into a strainer set over a bowl, then return the juice to the pan and simmer until reduced by half and thickened. Stir back into the rhubarb and leave to cool.

2 To make the syllabub, mix together the double cream, sugar, lemon juice and sherry. Using an electric mixer or by hand, whip the mixture until standing in soft peaks, then spoon into glasses and chill for an hour or so. To serve, spoon the rhubarb on top.

gooseberry fool

You can make this fool with other seasonal fruits, such as strawberries or raspberries, as well as plums and damsons. Sweet, soft fruits that don't need to be cooked can just be mashed up and folded through the whipped cream.

SERVES 4

150g (5oz) gooseberries, topped and tailed
50g (2oz) caster sugar, or more if needed
5 tablespoons dessert wine
juice of ¹/4 lemon
40g (1¹/2oz) caster sugar
250ml (8fl oz) double cream

1 Put the gooseberries, sugar and 2 tablespoons water into a pan and cook gently over a low heat for 10 minutes, to a jam-like consistency, Adjust the sweetness, then leave to cool.

2 Mix together the wine, lemon juice and sugar, add the cream and whip the mixture slowly until standing in soft peaks, using a whisk or an electric mixer. Fold in three quarters of the gooseberry compote, spoon into glasses and chill for 1–2 hours. Top with the rest of the fruit to serve.

burnt cream

Is this delicious dessert French or British in origin? It's difficult to say, as burnt cream seems to have been around for as long as *crème brûlée*. As far back as the Norman Conquest we have been influenced by the French and visa versa. Both versions may even be derived from the Spanish *crema Catalan*. Custard has always been the basis, and whoever had the idea of putting a mirror of burnt sugar on top deserves our eternal gratitude. There are lots of variations on the theme but, like most successful dishes, the simplest ones seem to work the best.

SERVES 4

600ml (1 pint) thick Jersey cream
8 medium egg yolks
75g (3oz) caster sugar

1 The day before serving, bring the cream to the boil and reduce by one third. Meanwhile, mix the egg yolks with 1 tablespoon of the caster sugar.

2 Pour the reduced cream on to the egg yolks and mix well, then return the mixture to the pan. Cook over a low heat, stirring constantly until the mixture coats the back of a spoon. Don't allow it to boil, or it will curdle. Remove from the heat.

3 Pour the mixture into 4 individual heatproof dishes, such as ramekins, and leave to cool. Chill overnight in the fridge.

4 An hour before serving, sprinkle an even layer of caster sugar over the cream and caramelise under a preheated hot grill or using a blow-torch.

jellies

simple fruit jelly

To serve 4, put 600ml (1 pint) bought or freshly pressed fruit juice and the juice of ½ lemon in a pan and bring to the boil. Add about 200g (7oz) caster sugar depending on sweetness of juice) and stir until dissolved; remove from heat. Soak 5 sheets leaf gelatine in cold water for a minute or until soft. Squeeze out the water, add to the syrup and stir until dissolved. Pour into 4 individual jelly moulds or one large one and chill to set.

For several years we've been serving jellies in the restaurants in various forms and flavoured with anything from Champagne to port (to serve with cheese, see page 169).

A simple fruit jelly can look very pretty, and is deceptively simple to make the day before a dinner party. To give your jelly a kick, add a good slug of kirsch, cassis or an appropriate fruit liqueur. You can vary the basic recipe by using different fresh fruit juices available in cartons, say strawberry, raspberry or a mixture, or even use diluted good quality fruit cordial. Puréed and sieved fresh berries also work well. Avoid acidic citrus fruit, pineapple and passion fruit juices, as these gradually break down the gelatine so the jelly just won't set.

To turn out a jelly, fill a bowl with almost boiling water, dip the moulds in briefly, then remove and loosen the jelly from the edge slightly with your finger. Turn the moulds over on to plates and carefully unmould.

▲ kids' jelly

Kids can have lots of fun with jelly at parties and you can make all sorts of shapes and colours for them, but do remember to leave out the alcohol. To prepare a child-friendly jelly, make a simple fruit jelly (as above), bearing in mind that some kids are fussy about certain sharp fruits. (You can always flavour it with cordial.) Set in fun moulds. Or you could even make little jelly sweets in ice cube moulds, with a single raspberry or blueberry set in it.

▼ elderflower jelly

You can make this with 6 freshly picked elderflower heads when they are available, or elderflower cordial. For a jelly to serve 4, put 400ml (14fl oz) water, 150ml (¼ pint) Sauternes or other good dessert wine and the juice of ½ lemon in a pan and bring to the boil. Add 200g (7oz) caster sugar and stir until dissolved, then remove from heat. If using the flower heads, rinse, pat dry and infuse them in the warm syrup

overnight. Next day, bring it to the boil again, remove and strain through a fine-meshed sieve. Soak 5 sheets leaf gelatine in a shallow bowl of cold water for a minute or so until soft. Squeeze out the water, add to the syrup and stir until dissolved. If using elderflower cordial, add 3 tablespoons at this stage. Pour the jelly into 4 individual jelly moulds or one large one and chill in the fridge to set. Turn out and serve.

▲ elderflower jelly with summer fruits

Make up the elderflower jelly (left) and leave to cool but don't let it set. Combine 150g (5oz) summer fruits (raspberries, blueberries, halved strawberries, etc). Divide half the fruit between 4 glasses, then pour in half the cooled, liquid jelly. Chill for an hour or so to set, then top up with the remaining fruits and liquid jelly. This keeps the fruits suspended in the jelly so they don't float to the top. Chill to set.

Eton mess with strawberries

This comforting summer dessert is so easy. Making the meringue is the most time-consuming part, so do this a day or two in advance, or cheat by buying 100–150g (3½–5oz) good quality ready-made meringue. Try it with different sweet berries during the summer months and, if you are lucky enough to have wild strawberries in your garden, scatter a few on top to show off a bit ...

SERVES 4

200g (7oz) ripe strawberries, hulled
100g (3½oz) caster sugar
500ml (16fl oz) double cream
few drops of vanilla extract

FOR THE MERINGUE:

1 medium egg white
65g (2½oz) caster sugar

1 To make the meringue, in a clean bowl, whisk the egg white until stiff, then gradually whisk in the caster sugar until the meringue forms stiff peaks when the whisk is lifted (use an electric mixer for best results).

2 Spread the meringue in an even layer, about 2 cm (¾ inch) thick, on a baking tray lined with greaseproof paper. Place in the oven at the lowest temperature setting and leave for about 6–7 hours until dry and brittle.

3 Put half of the strawberries into a blender with half of the sugar and whiz until smooth, then pass through a sieve to remove the seeds.

4 Whisk the double cream, remaining caster sugar and vanilla extract together in a bowl until stiff. Break the meringue into small pieces and fold into the cream with half of the strawberry purée. Don't mix it together too thoroughly; you want a ripple effect.

5 Slice the remaining strawberries. Spoon the cream mixture into the middle of each serving plate, then spoon most of the strawberry purée over and around the outside. Scatter the sliced strawberries on top and drizzle with the remaining strawberry purée to serve.

summer pudding

This is a good way to use a glut of summer fruit, though it also works well with frozen mixed fruits. Try to avoid a high proportion of blackcurrants, or similarly tart fruits, or you'll find the flavour too sour. If preferred, you can make single puddings, using individual pudding basins.

SERVES 4

900g (2lb) mixed summer fruits, such as strawberries (hulled and halved), raspberries, redcurrants, blueberries and blackberries

150g (5oz) caster sugar
about ½ large loaf good quality white bread

1   Put all the fruits and sugar into a saucepan, bring to a simmer and cook for 2 minutes to soften the fruit slightly, then leave to cool a little. (If using frozen fruit, drain off any juices after defrosting, then combine with the sugar, bring to a simmer and immediately remove from the heat.) Whiz about one sixth of the fruit and juice in a blender until smooth and set to one side to serve with the pudding.

2   Cut the bread into 5–8mm (¼–⅜ inch) thick slices and remove the crusts. Line a 1 litre (1¾ pint) pudding basin with cling film, allowing it to overhang the sides. Cut a circle from one slice of bread to fit the base. Cut the rest of the bread into pieces to fit around the sides and extend slightly above the rim, overlapping them slightly and pressing the joins together with your fingers.

3   Spoon the fruit and a little of the juice into the lined basin to come halfway up. Cover with a round of bread, then top up with the rest of the fruit and juice. Cut some more bread to fit the top and position, then fold the bread around the side over it a little. Bring the cling film up over the pudding and twist to seal. Cover with a plate and place a couple of tins (or something else heavy) on top to weight it down. Leave overnight in the fridge.

4   To serve, run a knife around the pudding to loosen it, hold a plate upside down on top and invert to turn out. Spoon the reserved fruit sauce over the pudding and serve, with some thick Jersey cream.

baked apples

Apple varieties such as large Cox's Orange Pippins, Braeburn or Jonagold work well for this dish, although apples can be a bit temperamental and react differently during cooking. It's a matter of how they were stored, as well as how ripe or unripe they are. You may have four apples in the oven from the same batch and one may take more or less time than the rest. The filling can be varied to taste with more or less spice, or the addition of nuts like ground almonds or walnuts.
Illustrated on previous page

SERVES 4
4 large apples (see above)
8 tablespoons luxury mincemeat

65g (2¹/₂oz) fresh white breadcrumbs
1 teaspoon ground cinnamon
2 tablespoons brown sugar

1 Preheat the oven to 190°C (fan oven 170°C), gas mark 5. Using an apple corer, scoop out the cores from the apples. Mix the mincemeat, breadcrumbs, cinnamon and sugar together. Put each apple on a larger piece of foil and fill the core cavities with the mincemeat mixture. Fold the foil up loosely around each apple and stand them on a baking tray.

2 Bake the apples in the oven for 45–60 minutes or until they are soft. Check them individually after 40 minutes, as the odd one may need removing before the rest if it cooks more quickly. Serve with custard (see right) or thick Jersey cream.

autumn fruits in mulled wine

This is a really simple dessert and makes good use of those blackberries that are a little tart to eat on their own. You can introduce other fruits instead of the pears and plums, such as apples and greengages.

SERVES 4
200ml (7fl oz) full-bodied fruity red wine (like a
* New World Merlot)*
1 small cinnamon stick
4 cloves
1 bay leaf

200g (7oz) brown sugar
few strips of orange peel
4 ripe plums
2 ripe pears
200g (7oz) blackberries, elderberries or
* blueberries*

1 Put the red wine into a pan with the cinnamon, cloves, bay leaf, sugar and orange peel. Bring to the boil and simmer gently for 5 minutes. Remove from the heat and leave to cool.

2 Meanwhile, quarter and stone the plums. Peel, halve and core the pears, then cut each half into 6 wedges. Put all the fruits in a bowl and pour the mulled wine over them. Cover and leave for at least 2 hours, stirring occasionally. Serve at room temperature, with thick Jersey cream.

pear and blackberry crumble

Crumbles are most usually associated with apples and rhubarb, but you can easily vary the fruits. Add some dried fruits in winter and scatter in berry fruits during the summer. The topping can also be jazzed up with the addition of oats or chunky pieces of nuts.

SERVES 4

6 large ripe pears
25g (1oz) unsalted butter
100g (3½oz) fresh or frozen blackberries
50–65g (2–2½oz) caster sugar
FOR THE CRUMBLE TOPPING:
75g (3oz) unsalted butter, diced
40g (1½oz) ground almonds
125g (4oz) caster sugar
160g (5½oz) plain flour

1 Preheat the oven to 180°C (fan oven 160°C), gas mark 4. Peel, core and roughly chop the pears. Melt the butter in a pan, add the pears and cook over a high heat, turning frequently, until soft and most of the liquid has evaporated. Add the blackberries and sugar to taste, stir until the sugar is dissolved and take off the heat.

2 To make the crumble topping, mix all the ingredients in a food processor or mixer, or rub between your fingers, until the mixture resembles breadcrumbs.

3 Fill a baking dish with the pear mixture and spoon the crumble evenly over the top. Bake for 20–30 minutes until the topping is golden brown. Serve with clotted cream or custard (below).

custard Split ½ vanilla pod in half lengthways and scrape out the seeds with the tip of a knife. Put 300ml (½ pint) single cream into a small saucepan with the vanilla pod and seeds and bring to the boil. Take off the heat and leave to infuse for 10 minutes, then remove the pod.
   In a bowl, mix together 5 medium egg yolks, 65g (2½oz) caster sugar and 2 teaspoons cornflour. Pour the cream on to the egg mixture, whisking well, then return to the pan. Cook gently over a low heat for a few minutes, stirring constantly with a wooden spoon until the custard thickens; don't let it boil or it may curdle. Remove from the heat and serve. This quantity is sufficient to serve 4.

Sussex pond pudding

This unusual pudding is steamed with a whole lemon inside that serves two purposes: one to hold the pudding up and secondly to permeate the rich buttery sauce with a delicate lemony flavour as it cooks. Once the pud is turned out on to the serving dish, it will be sitting in a pond of delicious sweet lemony sauce.

SERVES 4–6

250g (9oz) self-raising flour
125g (4oz) shredded beef suet
150ml (¼ pint) milk
200g (7oz) soft light brown sugar
300g (11oz) unsalted butter, softened
1 large unwaxed lemon

1 Mix the flour and suet together in a bowl, then gradually mix in the milk to form a dough. The dough should be soft but firm enough to roll out.

2 Roll out the dough to a circle large enough to line a 1.5 litre (2½ pint) pudding basin. Cut a quarter out of the circle for the lid and to ease the lining of the bowl. Butter the pudding basin well, drop the pastry into it and join up the edges where the quarter was removed.

3 Mix the sugar and butter together and put into the lined basin. With a roasting fork or skewer, prick the whole lemon all over as much as you can so that the juices can escape during cooking, then push it into the butter mixture.

4 Remould the pastry for the top and roll it out to the correct size. Lay it on top of the filling and press the edges together to seal in the filling. Cover the top of the basin with a generous piece of foil, making a pleat down the middle to allow for expansion. Secure in place under the rim with string, making a string handle so it can be lifted out easily.

5 Lower the pudding into a pan containing enough boiling water to come about halfway up the side of the basin. Cover and simmer for 4 hours, topping up with more boiling water as necessary.

6 To serve, lift out the basin and allow to stand for about 30 minutes, then remove the foil and loosen the sides with a small sharp knife. Put a deep serving dish over the basin and quickly turn the whole thing upside down – it may collapse a little but the flavour will be incredible.

spotted dick

This is one of the most popular comfort puddings from school days, public especially. It can be served with custard, or even more simply with golden syrup and a knob of butter. Spotted dick is one of the honoured members of the roly poly family and should be steamed. You can even buy cylindrical moulds for the purpose.

SERVES 4–6

360g (12¹/₂oz) plain flour
pinch of salt
2 teaspoons baking powder
180g (6¹/₄oz) suet
125g (4oz) soft brown sugar

175g (6oz) currants
grated zest of 1 lemon
¹/₂ teaspoon ground mixed spice
about 150ml (¹/₄ pint) milk
butter, to grease and serve
golden syrup, to serve

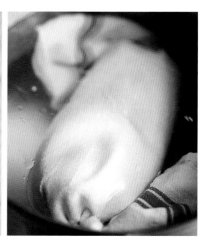

1 Sift the flour, salt and baking powder together into a large mixing bowl. Stir in the suet, sugar, currants, lemon zest and mixed spice, then add just enough milk to make a soft dough.

2 Shape the dough into a log shape and wrap loosely with buttered heavy-duty cling film. Wrap this loosely in muslin and secure with string. Drop into a large pan of boiling water and simmer for 2 hours. If using a cylindrical mould, line it with buttered greaseproof paper, put the dough in the mould and steam for 2¹/₂ hours.

3 To serve, remove the wrappings and cut the pudding into 3cm (1¹/₄ inch) slices. Serve with a knob of butter and drizzle with golden syrup.

sticky toffee pudding

To be successful, this addictive pudding must live up to its name. It's got to be sticky and gooey, and for that you need plenty of sauce between the layers to soak through and moisten them.

SERVES 4–6

150g (5oz) pitted dates
65g (2½oz) unsalted butter, plus extra to grease
175g (6oz) soft dark brown sugar
2 medium eggs, lightly beaten
225g (8oz) self-raising flour

FOR THE TOFFEE SAUCE:

600ml (1 pint) double cream
350g (12oz) caster sugar
90g (3¼oz) unsalted butter
:

1 Put the dates into a pan with 250ml (8fl oz) water and simmer over a low heat for 10–15 minutes or until the dates are soft and the water has almost evaporated. Whiz in a blender until smooth. The purée should be a good spoonable consistency; if too thick, thin with a little water. Leave to cool.

2 Preheat the oven to 180°C (fan oven 160°C), gas mark 4. Soften the butter. Grease a baking tin, measuring about 15x12x6cm (6x5x2½ inches), with butter and line with greaseproof paper.

3 To make the sponge, in a food processor, mixer or by hand, cream the butter and sugar together until light and fluffy. Add the eggs slowly, taking care that the mixture does not separate. (If this does happen, add a little of the flour and continue mixing for a minute or so.) Then gently fold in the flour, with a large metal spoon, until evenly mixed. Finally, fold in the date purée.

4 Spread the mixture in the baking tin and bake for about 50–60 minutes or until the sponge is firm to the touch. Allow to cool in the tin for 10 minutes or so. Keep the oven on.

5 Meanwhile, make the toffee sauce. Pour half of the cream into a heavy-based pan and add the sugar and butter. Bring to the boil, stirring, and continue to boil until the sauce is golden brown, 8–10 minutes or even longer. Allow to cool for about 10 minutes, then whisk in the remaining cream.

6 Remove the sponge from the tin, trim the edges to neaten, then cut horizontally into 4 even layers. Re-line the tin with fresh greaseproof paper. Reassemble the sponge in the tin, spreading two thirds of the warm sauce in between the layers. Reheat the pudding in the oven for 15–20 minutes.

7 To serve, cut the pudding into 4–6 portions, place in warm bowls and top with the remaining toffee sauce. Serve with ice cream, soured cream or crème fraîche.

apple charlotte

Many apple varieties were introduced in this country and then forgotten about in later years. The story goes that William Forsyth, gardener to George III, introduced the Beauty of Kent variety at the Brompton Park nurseries in the early 1800s. The new dessert was then named after the king's wife Charlotte, a patron of apple growers. Now it is made with cooking apples, of which Bramleys Seedling is probably the best known. You need to use a good quality sliced loaf or slice it yourself, or better still, use brioche. You may need to add more or less sugar depending on the sweetness of the apples.

SERVES 4

1.5kg (3¹/₄lb) Bramleys or other good
  cooking apples
140g (4¹/₂oz) unsalted butter
about 100g (3¹/₂oz) caster sugar
10–14 thin slices of good quality white bread
or brioche

1   Peel, quarter and core the apples, then cut into chunks. Melt 50g (2oz) of the butter in a heavy-based saucepan. Add the apples and sugar, cover and cook over a medium heat, stirring occasionally, for 8–10 minutes or so until softened. Remove the lid and cook until the liquid has evaporated and the apples are quite dry and cooked through but not puréed.

2   Preheat the oven to 200°C (fan oven 180°C), gas mark 6. Have ready 4 individual metal or foil pudding basins, measuring about 8–9cm (3¹/₄–3¹/₂ inches) across and 5–6cm (2–2¹/₂ inches) deep. Remove the crusts from the bread and melt the rest of the butter.

3   From each of 8 bread slices, cut a disc slightly smaller than the top of the pudding basins. Then cut 8 rectangular pieces of bread, about 7 x 12 cm (2³/₄ x 5 inches), from the other slices. These will line the walls of the basin, so the shorter side of the bread should be the same as the depth of the pudding basins, and 2 slices wrapped around the inside of the pudding bowl should overlap slightly.

4   To make the casing for the puddings, dip both sides of the bread rectangles in the melted butter and line the sides of each mould with two rectangular pieces, overlapping them slightly at the two joints. Dip the discs of bread into the butter on both sides and push one into the bottom of each mould with your fingers to fit snugly; make sure there aren't any gaps. Fill the moulds with the apple mixture. Top each with the 4 remaining bread discs, again dipped in butter, and pinch the edges of the bread together with your fingers to seal.

5   Cover the tops of the puddings loosely with foil and bake for 15 minutes. Turn the oven down to 170°C (fan oven 150°C), gas mark 3 and cook for a further 20 minutes. Turn each charlotte upside down on to a serving plate and leave covered with the mould for up to 20 minutes until ready to serve. Remove the moulds and serve the charlottes with thick spooning cream or clotted cream.

rice pudding with vanilla apricots

Rice pudding is easily adapted to suit different palates depending on how wet or stodgy everyone likes it, and whether you want a sophisticated twist, like the vanilla apricot compote here, or just good old jam. When fresh apricots are out of season, use ready-to-eat dried apricots and soak them overnight in warm water to cover.

SERVES 4

100g (3¹/₂oz) pudding rice
50g (2oz) caster sugar
pinch of freshly grated nutmeg
600ml (1 pint) full-fat milk
100ml (3¹/₂fl oz) double cream
150ml (¹/₄ pint) evaporated milk

FOR THE APRICOT COMPOTE:
¹/₂ vanilla pod
25g (1oz) unsalted butter
25g (1oz) caster sugar
12 ripe apricots, halved and stoned

1 Put the rice, caster sugar, nutmeg and full-fat milk into a pan, bring to the boil and simmer for 20 minutes or until the rice is tender, stirring from time to time.

2 Add the cream and evaporated milk, bring back a simmer and cook gently for another 10 minutes. Remove from the heat. If serving cold, set aside to cool.

3 To make the apricot compote, split the vanilla pod in half lengthways and scrape out the seeds with the tip of a knife. Put the butter and sugar into a saucepan with the vanilla and 1 tablespoon water. Simmer for about 5 minutes until the sugar has melted and the mixture has thickened. Add the apricots, cover with a lid and cook for 10 minutes. Remove from the heat and leave to cool.

4 Serve the rice pudding with the apricot compote, either hot or cold.

the classic British cheeseboard

These days we are gently persuading ourselves to indulge in a little cheese before dessert, as opposed to after it, or even in some cases instead of it. I personally don't mind either way, though a plate of cheese on the dinner table after dessert can sometimes be a good way to finish up the red wine. In France, of course, cheese after dessert is unheard of and there is no choice in the matter. So don't be pushed into it by cheese snobs.

Cheese-makers in the British Isles are now making some amazing cheeses, and always have, but until recently there hasn't been the commercial demand for them and restaurants have tended to offer a 'French-only' cheeseboard, with maybe a token Stilton. I remember, as a kid, hearing about Blue Vinney and how difficult it was to get hold of. Now, of course, it sits on supermarket shelves alongside other well-made English blues, like Jersey and Yorkshire blue. The array of English goat's cheeses now available includes fresh creamy ones and hard matured cheeses that match up to any in the world.

The Irish seem to have grasped the whole business of cheesemaking and I would happily sit confronted with a plate of Duras, Coleeney and Cashel Blue, among others. Cheeses of the British Isles should be of top eating quality, because we have such good dairy products and first-class milk with which to produce them.

Salad doesn't complement our semi-hard to hard cheeses in the same way it does the soft French cheeses. Chutneys and pickles are our *pièces de resistance*, and crisp celery doesn't go amiss. Recently I have started to complement cheeses with jellies. Blackcurrant jelly is the perfect match for Stilton and similar British blue cheeses, like Harbourne Blue and Yorkshire Blue, or the French Roquefort. Port jelly is exceptional with Stilton. Surprise your guests with a pot when you bring out the Stilton at Christmas.

blackcurrant jelly Place 450g (1lb) blackcurrants (or blackberries) and 450g (1lb) caster sugar sugar in a large heavy-based saucepan and gently bring to the boil, stirring. Skim off any scum that rises to the surface and simmer for 1 hour. Pass through a fine sieve, pour into two sterilised 450g (1lb) jars and leave to set. Store in the fridge for up to 2 months.

port jelly Soak 3 sheets leaf gelatine in cold water to cover. Meanwhile, put 600ml (1 pint) port, 1 clove, 1 cinnamon stick and 65g (2½oz) sugar in a saucepan, bring to the boil and reduce to about 400ml (14fl oz). Squeeze out excess water from the gelatine leaves and dissolve them in the hot liquid. Pass through a fine sieve, allow to cool, then store in a sterilised jar in the fridge for up to 2 months.

8 teatime

scones

These are at the heart of a West Country cream tea, topped with clotted cream and strawberry jam. The basic recipe can be varied by adding raisins or currants, and even some grated lemon rind or mixed chopped candied peel. Scones are best eaten on the day they are made, though they can be frozen and warmed through when you have friends or family round for tea.

MAKES 12

225g (8oz) plain flour, plus extra to dust
2 teaspoons baking powder
50g (2oz) butter, cut into small pieces
pinch of salt
1 teaspoon sugar
about 150ml (1/4 pint) milk

TO SERVE:
clotted cream
strawberry or other jam (preferably homemade)

1 Preheat the oven to 220°C (fan oven 200°C), gas mark 7. Sift the flour and baking powder together into a mixing bowl, then rub in the butter until the mixture has the texture of breadcrumbs. Stir in the salt and sugar, then slowly mix in just enough milk to form a stiff dough.

2 Gently roll out the dough on a floured surface to a 1.5–2cm (5/8–3/4 inch) thickness. Cut out rounds, using a 6–7cm (2½–2¾ inches) plain cutter. Arrange well apart on a baking sheet and bake for 10–15 minutes until well risen and golden.

3 Transfer the cooked scones to a wire rack and allow to cool slightly. Serve them warm, with clotted cream and jam.

drop scones

Also called Scotch pancakes, these drop scones are appropriately named because the mixture is literally dropped from the spoon directly on to the griddle. They are delicious served warm with butter, but even better I think topped with a spoonful of berry compote.

MAKES 8–12

225g (8oz) plain flour
1/2 teaspoon bicarbonate of soda
1/2 teaspoon cream of tartar
50g (2oz) granulated sugar
2 medium eggs, beaten
about 275ml (9fl oz) milk
a little oil, to grease pan

TO SERVE:
fruit compote or fresh berries and cream,
  or soft butter

1 Sift the flour, bicarbonate of soda and cream of tartar into a large mixing bowl, then add the sugar. Stir in the eggs and enough of the milk to form a smooth batter.

2 Heat a griddle pan or non-stick frying pan and oil it lightly. Drop spoonfuls of the mixture into the pan, spacing them well apart to allow for expansion. Let them cook for 3 minutes until bubbles rise to the surface, then turn the scones over and cook for another 2–3 minutes. Remove and place on some kitchen paper to drain. Keep warm while you cook the rest, wiping the pan and greasing with oil again for each batch.

3 Serve the drop scones warm, with fruit compote or fresh berries and cream, or just some butter.

shortbread

Originally from Scotland, shortbread has lots of variations, from the additions of rice flour in some parts of Scotland to demerara sugar in Dorset, and caraway and coriander in the similar Goosnargh cakes of Lancashire.

MAKES ABOUT 8–12 PIECES

480g (1lb 1oz) plain flour, plus extra to dust
125g (4oz) caster sugar

360g (12 ½oz) unsalted butter, cut into
  small pieces
2 medium eggs, beaten

1 Mix the flour and sugar together in a bowl, then rub in the butter with your fingertips until the mixture resembles breadcrumbs. Make a well in the centre and add the beaten eggs. Mix well to form a smooth dough.

2 Transfer the dough to a lightly floured surface. Roll out to a thickness of about 5mm (¼ inch) or thicker if you wish, in a round or rectangle (depending on the shape required). Mark into wedges or fingers and prick all over with a fork.

3 Transfer the shortbread to a baking tray and chill for about 30 minutes. Meanwhile, preheat the oven to 180°C (fan oven 160°C), gas mark 4. Bake the shortbread for 15–20 minutes or until lightly coloured. Dust with caster sugar while still warm. Store in an airtight container until required.

afternoon tea

A good afternoon tea, with its platters of delicate sandwiches followed by selections of cakes and pastries, is expected of a fine hotel. Tea at the Ritz or Waldorf, for example, is part of London's tradition, helping to break up a shopping trip, or providing a good meeting point to catch up with old friends.

Out of the cities, at teahouses, thatched inns and seaside cafes, afternoon tea is offered in various forms, like the famous West Country cream tea – warm scones topped with a good spoonful of clotted cream and homemade strawberry jam.

Cucumber sandwiches are traditional afternoon tea fare, first served with tea when it became a fashionable drink in the early 1800s. Watercress and egg mayonnaise sandwiches, too, can be quite delicious. Freshly baked bread is a good starting point and naturally, good farmhouse butter. Serve sandwiches, with or without crusts, on your best china to impress your tea guests.

▲ **egg mayonnaise sandwiches**
Boil the best free-range eggs for about 4 minutes, so the yolk is just cooked. Cool under cold running water, enough to be able to shell them. Spike some good quality mayonnaise (ideally homemade, page 45) with a little English mustard. Chop your eggs, fold in the mayonnaise and season with salt and black pepper. Serve on wholemeal or Granary bread and add a few chopped watercress leaves, if you wish. Allow 1 egg, plus a small spoonful of mayo per sandwich round.

watercress sandwiches

Watercress has an amazing freshness with a little kick of heat, which makes it perfect between two slices of bread. Don't trim, just rinse and dry. Piled thickly between buttered slices of good white or brown bread, with a little sea salt, it makes a perfect sandwich. If you want to be adventurous, though, try adding some crayfish (sold shelled in brine) to the watercress, or cooked, peeled prawns, mixed with a little mayonnaise.

cucumber sandwiches

Halve, deseed and thinly slice the cucumber, but don't peel it. Scatter the slices on a tray, season lightly with fine sea salt and leave for 10 minutes, then pat dry with kitchen paper. As the salt draws moisture out, it concentrates the flavour. Season the cucumber with black pepper and sandwich between good bread – light caraway bread is perfect. If liked, spread with a little cream cheese, though the flavour is sufficient without.

▲ scones with cream and jam

These are associated with cream teas throughout the British Isles. Scones are easy to make and taste far better bought ones (see recipe, page 173). Clotted cream is traditional in the West Country. It's made from rich, creamy local milk, which is scalded slowly over steam. The cream rises to the top of the pan as it cools and forms a thick yellow crust. This is skimmed off and sold as clotted cream.

▲ cucumber and salmon sandwiches

If you want something more substantial, some hot-smoked salmon, freshly poached salmon or trout, or cooked crab-meat, bound with a little mayonnaise mixed with a squeeze of lemon and some chopped dill would be a modest addition to the cucumber sandwiches (above).

Eccles cakes

Named after the small town on the outskirts of Manchester where they were first made, eccles cakes are delicious eaten on their own, but they also go well with hard cheeses, like Lancashire. They are traditionally made with flaky pastry, as here, but puff pastry is a suitable alternative.

MAKES 12–15

225g (8oz) plain flour, plus extra to dust

pinch of salt

90g (3¼oz) butter, frozen

90g (3¼oz) lard, frozen

TO GLAZE:

2 medium egg whites

caster sugar, to sprinkle

FOR THE FILLING:

75g (3oz) butter

150g (5oz) soft brown sugar

150g (5oz) currants

1 teaspoon ground cinnamon

½ teaspoon freshly grated nutmeg

grated zest of 1 orange

50g (2oz) chopped mixed candied peel

1   To make the pastry, sift the flour and salt into a bowl, then coarsely grate the frozen butter and lard over the flour. Distribute the fats evenly through the flour, using a metal spoon. Add just enough cold water to form a pliable dough, then wrap in cling film and refrigerate for 30 minutes.

2   Meanwhile, make the filling: melt the butter in a pan and mix it with all the other ingredients. Preheat the oven to 220°C (fan oven 200°C), gas mark 7.

3   Roll the pastry out on a floured surface to a 3mm (⅛ inch) thickness. Cut out rounds, using a plain 9cm (3½ inch) cutter. Put a heaped teaspoon of filling in the centre of each round and brush the edge of half the circle with a little water. Draw the edges up over the filling and pinch together to resemble an old-fashioned purse.

4   Turn the 'purses' over, then gently flatten with a rolling pin and cut a slit in the top of each one. Brush with egg white, sprinkle with caster sugar and bake for 15 minutes. Serve just warm.

hot cross buns

This most popular of Easter breads is traditionally baked and eaten on Good Friday, and it is the only British bread to retain the symbolic cross as a decoration. To enjoy hot cross buns at their best, serve them warm, split and buttered.

Illustrated on previous page

MAKES 20

650g (1lb 7oz) strong plain flour, plus extra
   to dust
1 teaspoon ground cinnamon
1 teaspoon freshly grated nutmeg
1 teaspoon ground mixed spice
1/2 teaspoon ground mace
1/2 teaspoon salt
65g (2 1/2oz) caster sugar
90g (3 1/4oz) butter
7g (1/4oz) sachet fast-action dried yeast
200ml (7fl oz) warm milk
200ml (7fl oz) hot water
1 medium egg, beaten
100g (3 1/2oz) raisins
65g (2 1/2oz) chopped mixed candied peel

TO FINISH:

1 medium egg, beaten
40g (1 1/2oz) plain flour
few drops of almond extract
65g (2 1/2oz) caster sugar
6 cubes of white sugar, coarsely crushed

1 Sift the flour, spices and salt into a warm mixing bowl and stir in the sugar. Rub in the butter and stir in the dried yeast. Add the warm milk, hot water and egg, and mix to a soft dough. Knead the dough by stretching and folding it for about 10 minutes on a lightly floured surface.

2 Knead the raisins and mixed peel into the dough, then roll the dough into a long sausage shape. Cut into 20 discs with a knife, then shape these into buns. Place them, at least 5cm (2 inches) apart, on a baking tray lined with greaseproof paper. Cover with cling film and leave to prove in a warm place for 30 minutes. Preheat the oven to 230°C (fan oven 210°C), gas mark 8.

3 Remove the cling film and brush the buns with the beaten egg. Mix the flour to a paste with a little water and the almond extract. Put into a piping bag and pipe a wide cross on top of each bun.

4 Bake the buns for 15 minutes, then transfer to a rack to cool. While they are still warm, mix the caster sugar and crushed sugar cubes with 5 tablespoons water. Brush the buns with this mixture and leave to cool completely.

lardy cake

The amount of lard, sugar and fruit in this traditional pastry varies in different recipes from around the country, and you can put in more or less, depending on your taste. It is essential, though, to serve lardy cake slightly warm, ideally still fresh from the oven.

MAKES ABOUT 12 SQUARES
650g (1lb 7oz) strong white bread flour
2 teaspoons salt
1 teaspoon caster sugar, plus extra to sprinkle
7g (1/4oz) sachet fast-action dried yeast
400ml (14fl oz) warm water
200g (7oz) lard, softened
50g (2oz) butter, softened
200g (7oz) mixed dried fruit
75g (3oz) chopped mixed candied peel
200g (7oz) granulated sugar

1   In a warm mixing bowl, mix the flour, salt, sugar and yeast. Add the warm water and mix to a soft dough. Knead the dough by stretching and folding it for about 10 minutes on a lightly floured surface.

2   Mix the lard, butter, fruit, peel and granulated sugar together and divide into 3 portions. On a lightly floured surface, roll out the bread dough to a rectangle, roughly three times as long as it is wide. Spread two thirds of its length with one batch of the lard mixture, then fold both long ends of the dough into the centre and firmly press the edges with your fingers or the rolling pin. Repeat this process twice more, using up the lard mixture.

3   Put the dough into a shallow baking tin with enough room for it to rise. Leave to prove in a warm place for about 30 minutes. Meanwhile, preheat the oven to 190°C (fan oven 170°C), gas mark 5.

4   Bake the lardy cake for about 45 minutes. Turn it out upside down on to another tray or large dish and leave to cool a little. Sprinkle the cake generously with caster sugar. Serve while still warm, cut into generous squares.

Victoria sandwich cake

Named after Queen Victoria, this is also sometimes referred to as a Victoria sponge. I have vivid memories of the Victoria sponge that my grandmother used to make twice a week. It would normally be sandwiched together with jam and occasionally butter cream. You can really use your imagination and fill it with other lovely things, like crushed berries and cream in the summer, or even sweetened cream cheese and fruit.

MAKES AN 18CM (7 INCH) SPONGE

150g (5oz) butter, at room temperature, plus extra to grease
150g (5oz) caster sugar
3 medium eggs, beaten
few drops of vanilla extract
150g (5oz) self-raising flour, sifted

FILLING:
strawberry or raspberry jam, or whipped cream and raspberries or strawberries

TO SERVE:
icing sugar, to dust

1 Preheat the oven to 170°C (fan oven 150°C), gas mark 3 and butter two 18cm (7inch) sandwich tins, 2.5cm (1 inch) deep. Line the bases with greaseproof paper.

2 In a large mixing bowl with a wooden spoon or electric mixer, cream the butter and sugar together until you get a pale mixture that drops off a spoon easily. Add the eggs a little at a time, beating the mixture thoroughly after each addition. Stir in the vanilla extract.

3 Sift the flour into the bowl in 4 stages, each time gently folding it in with a large metal spoon to keep the mixture light. The mixture should again drop off a spoon easily.

4 Divide the mixture between the tins and cook on the centre shelf of the oven for 25–30 minutes. To test if the sponges are cooked, gently press your finger on the top and the imprint will spring back to shape. Leave the sponges in the tins for a couple minutes, then run a knife around the edge and turn them out on to wire cooling racks. Leave to cool completely.

5 To assemble, spread one of the sponge rounds with the jam, or whipped cream and berries. Place the other sponge round on top and press firmly. Dust with icing sugar to serve.

Madeira cake

This 19th-century cake was traditionally served with a glass of Madeira, hence the name. It's less fashionable now, but still a good, simple teatime cake.

MAKES A 20CM (8 INCH) CAKE

175g (6oz) butter, at room temperature, plus
  extra to grease
175g (6oz) caster sugar

4 medium eggs, beaten
grated zest of 1/2 lemon
275g (10oz) plain flour
1/2 teaspoon baking powder

1   Preheat the oven to 180°C (fan oven 160°C), gas mark 4 and line a 20cm (8 inch) cake tin with buttered greaseproof paper. In a mixing bowl with a wooden spoon or electric mixer, cream the butter and sugar together until you get a pale mixture that drops off a spoon easily. Add the eggs a little at a time, beating the mixture thoroughly after each addition. Stir in the grated lemon zest.

2   Sift the flour and baking powder together and add it to the mixture in 4 stages, each time gently folding it in with a metal spoon to keep the mixture light. Spoon the mixture into the prepared cake tin and bake for 1 1/2 hours. Leave in the tin for 10 minutes or so, then turn out and cool on a wire rack.

banana bread

The bananas ensure that this teabread stays nice and moist for a few days. It is delicious served just as it is, or topped with jam.

MAKES ABOUT 20 SLICES

90g (3 1/4oz) butter, melted, plus extra to grease
240g (8 1/2oz) plain flour
1 teaspoon salt
1 teaspoon baking powder
1 teaspoon ground cinnamon

125g (4oz) caster sugar
1 medium egg, beaten
few drops of vanilla extract
100g (3 1/2oz) pecan nuts, chopped
4 ripe bananas, peeled and mashed

1   Preheat the oven to 190°C (fan oven 170°C), gas mark 5 and lightly butter a loaf tin. Sift the flour, salt, baking powder and cinnamon into a mixing bowl and stir in the sugar. Gently mix in the egg, butter and vanilla, then fold in the nuts and bananas.

2   Turn the mixture into the loaf tin and bake for 40–50 minutes, until a skewer inserted in the centre comes out dry. Leave in the tin for 10 minutes before turning out on a wire rack to cool completely.

Dundee cake

This recipe is for a lighter version than some of those heavy fruit cakes that get left at Christmas time. The story goes that Dundee cake was created by the famous marmalade makers of Dundee, Keillers, to use up excess citrus rind when they were not producing marmalade.

MAKES AN 18CM (7 INCH) CAKE

150g (5oz) butter, at room temperature, plus
    extra to grease
150g (5oz) caster sugar
3 medium eggs, beaten
225g (8oz) plain flour
1 teaspoon baking powder
175g (6oz) currants

175g (6oz) sultanas
50g (2oz) glacé cherries, rinsed, dried and halved
50g (2oz) mixed candied peel, finely chopped
2 tablespoons ground almonds
grated zest of 1 lemon
grated zest of 1 orange
about 25g (1oz) whole blanched almonds

1 Preheat the oven to 170°C (fan oven 150°C), gas mark 3 and butter a deep 18–20cm (7–8 inch) round cake tin, then line it with greaseproof paper.

2 In a mixing bowl using a wooden spoon or electric mixer, cream the butter and sugar together until you get a pale mixture that drops off a spoon easily. Add the eggs a little at a time, beating the mixture thoroughly after each addition.

3 Sift the flour and baking powder together. Add it to the mixture in 4 stages, each time gently folding it in with a large metal spoon to keep the mixture light. Again, the mixture should drop off a spoon easily.

4 Gently fold in the rest of the ingredients, except for the whole almonds, and spoon the mixture into the cake tin, spreading it evenly with the back of a spoon. Carefully arrange the whole almonds on the top in a circle; do not press them in though, or they will sink during baking. Bake the cake on the middle shelf of the oven for 2–2½ hours, or until it looks firm and the top feels springy to the touch.

5 Leave the cake to cool in the tin, then run a knife around the edge to loosen and remove to a wire rack. When cold, transfer to an airtight container. Dundee cake is best allowed to mature for a couple days before cutting.

index